T0130198

PARENTS…

YOUR HS TEENS HAVE BEEN REPLACED BY ALIENS!

BY SENIOR DEPUTY O'DELL P. GLENN

Order this book online at www.trafford.com
or email orders@trafford.com

Most Trafford titles are also available at major online book retailers.

Printed in the United States of America.

ISBN: 978-1-4269-4709-4 (sc)
ISBN: 978-1-4269-4710-0 (e)

Library of Congress Control Number: 2010916672

Trafford rev. 11/06/2010

 www.trafford.com

North America & international
toll-free: 1 888 232 4444 (USA & Canada)
phone: 250 383 6864 ♦ fax: 812 355 4082

ACKNOWLEDGEMENTS

This Book is dedicated to my beautiful alien teen daughter, Zahtia Ashleigh Glenn…love you.

Thank you to the following friends, family, and co-workers who make my life a living hell, just kidding;

Thomas, Lynda, Cynthia, Dianne, Lisa, Gail, Joanie, Libby, Sheriff Lott & RCSD, Mr. Price & BHS, Mr. Greene, The Sanders Middle School Crew, My Guys night out Crew, Dan & Fitz, and B Squad.

…and in the words of Mr. Te-Mony, "Some people think it, but Deputy Glenn says it."

INTRODUCTION

Okay, so you decided to buy this book because you are actually curious about what kind of insight some school cop might have about your teen. You have made a wise decision in selecting this book over the latest political diatribe. Besides you already know the state of world affairs, they suck.

ALIEN TEEN CHAPTERS

Introduction

You may wonder, why in the hell is a Sheriff's Deputy writing a book when there is so much crime going on in America today. Well, believe it or not, those same people that are committing those crimes are our children, family members and even that uncle you don't claim.

But that's another issue. This book is to warn you, the parents of teens, that your High School Teens have been replaced by Aliens. Mine included. The bad thing is, we didn't know about the switch. Lord, I long for the return of my precious little girl. Wherever she is out there in space, I hope they take good care of her.

When you read this book, it will amuse, tickle, anger, and sometimes make you shake your head and wonder, "where are the parents to these teens." The parents are right here and they are you. Only now you will have some insight to how your teen's mind function.

Look, haven't you wondered why all of a sudden, you don't understand a damn thing your teen is saying to you. Ever notice that they avoid you when they are with friends. Ever wonder what they are doing for so long in the family bathroom? You know you have. When you try to talk to them, ever notice they give you that same look your pet dog gives you, kind of a blank, head tilted stare?

On a serious note, my main focus in writing this book is to bring to your attention, parents, that we really don't know our teens. We would like to think we do, but when in the high school, or their social setting, they are totally different individuals. That's not to say that all teens turn from Jekyll to Hyde when they are out of your sights, but their "real" personalities take flight when released from your gaze.

Chapter 1

Freshies, who needs 'em

Ah it's the first day of school at Anywhere High School located in Anywhere USA. Would you believe this high school is designed to hold 2,200 of our precious teenagers? Funny thing is, there must be almost 2,400 students coming here to try and get an education.

Aside from the educational aspect, all of these hormone driven Teen freshmen are here to try and get laid. That's right, laid. Not that they really know what that means. During middle school, they caught a glimpse of some T & A when they sneaked and watched dad's porn collection. They may have been passing your room when you and your spouse were doing the "wild monkey thing." You forgot to close the door completely. Totally screwed up your teen's perspective on life.

Whatever the case, here they are. Man, there must be over 700 Freshies crowding into the lobby of the school. Some are in the food court and some lingering outside around the building. All you hear is chatter, chatter, chatter. I doubt that they know what they are talking about. So what, it still makes them look cool, now that they are big time high schoolers.

What's funny is that they don't notice how the upper classmen are making faces at these little cherry faced, noisy things swarming all over the place. There is almost a look of disgust on their faces as they try to squeeze through this massive horde of Freshies. Honestly, makes you want to just grab one and put him into a nearby garbage can. Yeah, that would be so cool.

Let's see what we have here, hmm, there is the former eighth grader still wearing last years sneakers. He's gonna be dead meat when the bullies get a hold of him. Not to mention, he has enough jell in his hair to grease the axle of a car.

Over there is a cute little girl with all of her A-cup size chest hanging out. No breasts, just all nipples. She is wearing the "in" style of mini dresses. The latest style is billowy from the waist down, then tight at the bottom five inches of the dress. Probably would look great on a real woman. Wonder if her mom got a chance to see her before she left the house. Probably not. I'm sure she will get the attention of the assistant principal, Dr. I. Hateeverthing. She is the designated fashion police of this school.

Over there are the so-called cool teens. They're the black guys who have a little bit of size to them and probably played football in middle school. They all gravitate towards each other worst then girls do. They even cackle and cluck just as much. They seem to be talking about how they will be starting on the varsity football team because they are that good. Boy are they going to get a rude awakening when coach get them on the field and show them what the real deal is. Some will make the junior varsity team, some will fade away like a bad memory or a hangover. That's nature's law of the fit ruling the roost.

There is my group of freshie Diva's. You know, the girl with all of the long hair, big boobs and ass for days. You remember those girls don't you ladies? You wanted to scratch their eyes out and set their hair on fire. Although with all of the weave they are wearing, that would be a hell of a blaze.

They always pretend they are involved in the conversation they are having within their group, but actually, they are posing and styling for the crowd. See there, see how she just tossed her head back and swung the hair around. How does she make her hair move in slow motion like that? Ah the Diva's are in effect.

Oh my God, look over there huddled in the corner of the lobby, cowering, sweating, and afraid to look around at their new home. It's the nerdy, book-smart, can relate to a WII game system kids. They are so precious in their fear. God, I sure hope they didn't dress themselves. You should know you can't mix stripes with checks. Funny thing is, somewhere along this new trek they are embarking on, some of these same goofy looking freshies will actually blossom into a real young adult. Others will not and will be thrown into the lake in front of the school to feed the catfish.

The teachers and administration people are out in force today. By the look on some of their faces, they are dreading having to be locked inside four walls with this mass of zits and tits. They all look as if they are ready to make a rush for the door and not have to put up with these fresh new students.

You ever notice how no matter what, the principal always manages to smile and shake hands and crack jokes with all of the students he comes in contact with. You would too if you only had to deal with them for a brief minute each day. Not quite like being locked in a cage with a hungry tiger. Yes, principals have it made in the shade.

To be honest with you, I have it made also. You know that as a SRO, which is a School Resource Officer, we have more authority over the school and the personnel than the principal.

That's right. We have the constitutional authority to enforce the laws of the land. We can actually remove, arrest the principal, if the need be. Fortunately, that is the last thing we are here to do.

We are actually here as mentors, role models, teachers, protectors, punishers, and most of all, a friend in deed. The latter is one I take very seriously. When a child's parent has gotten to the point where they don't want to listen, then there are us. Your friendly neighborhood Spider-man, I mean Deputy.

Back to the Freshies. There is the first bell, time for all other students to find their homeroom classes and start the business of the day. For teachers, that's finding out who the hell they have gotten stuck with for the rest of the year.

You know every year all high schools have a before year orientation in which the future freshmen come to the school with their parents and actually find their way around their new school. As we know, freshmen's use their minds and memories the same way a bull use his tits. They don't! So that is why we have a ball of confusion jam-packed in all of the hallways trying to go three ways all at once. Talk about something out of a three stooge's movie.

Sooner rather than later, they all finally find their classes. Now begins the task of the teachers to make sure they have the body that is supposed to be assigned to them. Fifteen minutes later, there are still freshies walking around in the hallways in circles trying to find a place to call their own. Poor things, come on here, I will help you find some place to go. Poor little freshies seems to have forgotten how to read. It happens.

Now you have got to be kidding me. Why are all of you parents still hanging around the school. Look, you did your job and brought your little bundle of alien joy to the school in your fancy new SUV, so now, be gone. Nothing to see here. It was bad enough that you parent created a helluva traffic jam as you drove your alien high school teen to school this morning. Now you are hanging around the outside of the building, trying to look in and see your child.

You guys have got to let go of the alien teens. Come on, pull that titty out of their mouths and let them fend for themselves. They will be alright. We get paid a nice salary to ensure that your alien teen spends quality time with us and then are returned to you. Hopefully in better condition then when you brought them to us.

Oh lord, why do all of you parents have soccer stickers on the sides of the family car. Now Ms. Simpkins, you know full well that your child, Matt, is too damn fat to play soccer. Then again, I have seen how fast he can move when the lunch bell rings. But still, take that soccer stick-on off of your car, you ain't fooling anybody. Please.

You know it never ceases to amaze me how some parents seem to not want to let go of their children. Even though they have been replaced by alien's bodies, some moms and dads will continue to chauffer their teen all the way to college.

So what is wrong with putting their asses on the bus? Think about it, you may even get a few more minutes of snooze time if they take the bus. Moms, why do you persist in scaring people with those crazy rollers stuck in your hair as you drive up to the School. That funk old bathrobe ain't doing anything for our opinion of you either.

A lot of tax dollars are paid each year to ensure a big yellow limousine will come right to your house and take your little nestling to school for you. Why not take advantage of that service?

Every day you will see almost three hundred to four hundred cars turning into this high school. They actually caused the highway department and department of transportation to have to widen the road to accommodate all of the car-riders coming to the school. You talk about a traffic jam, this is it.

Parents treat their freshies as if they were going to the first grade all over again. It is almost like a festival event with the parade of SUV's, vans, and expensive cars that will drop their loads off at the school.

Mama, you know you can drop your alien teenager off along the side of the school building and they can actually walk to the front door. Oh, you would rather drive them to the front of the school instead. Are you afraid that if you drop him off on the side of the building, he might haul ass through the parking lot and run into the woods, never to be heard from again? You car pool parents kill me. Let them walk the last 15 yards. It won't kill or hurt them. Oh no, you have to ensure they go through the front door.

Mom, I have news for you. Do you realize that there are hundreds of other doors to this school and just because you want to see them enter the school, doesn't mean they won't escape out of another door before your tail lights turn the corner? Didn't think that far ahead, did you freshie parent.

Truth be known, freshies couldn't find their way out of the school if you lead them by the hands. Look at them, they are so wide eyed and scared as hell. Some of them are playing it off pretty good. If I walk up behind you and go "boo," right about now, we probably would need a janitor to clean up the mess you dropped from your pants.

Every time the bell rings, everyone get exactly 6 minutes to get to the next class. That is a very easy concept. Even though this school seems like miles of hallways, I and the principal have easily made it to each class in about 3 ½ minutes. That's walking with a purpose and not dicking around or horse playing.

At that kind of timing, you have actually got enough time to almost walk your girlfriend to class, get your kiss on and haul ass to your own class without any problem.

As we all know, there is no danger of your alien freshie kissing anything except the back of his or her own hand when they practice kissing. Who in their right mind would kiss a freshie anyway? They still slobber and pop spit when they talk. Can't put your lips on that kind of moisture.

School usually has a full assembly in the gym or the auditorium so they can lay the smack down to all of the newbies. This is a do's and don't session. They break out the video and each administrator gets a chance to speak to the freshies.

As the local SRO, I get my turn and the freshies always seem more interested in what I have to say then the school officials. I think that's because I try to make my presentation more entertaining then they do.

For example, I speak about how illegal it is to bring a gun into the school. I carry a plastic 9mm gun in my "bag of goodies" to do my demonstrations when I teach classes. That 9mm has a laser light on it just like the real thing. During my lecture, I will pull the gun out to demonstrate what not to bring. The laser light "accidentally" comes on as it inadvertently points towards the audience.

You can always tell street-smarts kids from sheltered kids with a simple trick of the fake handgun. When the laser light appeared on the chest or head of an alien freshie in the audience, you should see how quickly they duck and dodge. They really become unnerved when that laser beam is on their body. Street-smart teen's ducks, sheltered teen simply looks in wonderment. Oooohhhhhh ooooooo… they are so silly.

Believe me, when I pull out my big bag of "weed," you can just hear the murmurs run rampant through the crowd. These alien teens have seen, come in contact with, used, or sold this shit before. Parents you need to understand that "your" child would not sell marijuana. But you don't have your original child, you have an alien teen and he or she will sell weed like Microsoft sells video games. Don't fool yourself by thinking that they won't.

Mom and Dad, don't let the fact that your alien freshie has been living in your house for so long that you think you know them. I am never surprise when I have to arrest an alien teen for possessing marijuana. You want to stand there and argue with me that it was someone else's fault. HELLO, your alien teen had the weed in his drawers and I don't think anyone else stuck their hands in his wiener "holder" to put the drugs there. Wake up McFly, wake up.

The briefing went very well and I think ¾ of the alien teens understand that if your violate the rules, then you are ass-out. The other ¼ of the alien population will test the system and get kicked out of school, and end up pushing a broom the rest of their life. Alien freshies are kind of stupid. Tell them the stove is hot, and that's like giving them an invitation to sit their asses on the burner to find out.

The first day usually goes off without much problems, but it never fails, there are a few girls here that are carrying over grudges they had with each other in middle school.

I hate girl drama. Especially alien- freshie girl drama. They want to fight over the stupidest things that don't matter. And parents, you need to stop telling those alien teen girls that "if someone hits you, you better hit them back." The only thing that will happen is that your alien teen girl will be looking you in the face for a few days while she is suspended. That wasn't good advice after all. Cut it out.

We will talk more about the girl fight thing a little later. Now it's time to put these alien freshies asses on the buses and in the cars they came here in. It's the end of the day. Wait a minute, why don't they leave? They are just lingering around in the lobby, hands waving, mouths moving a mile a minute, laughing, giggling and not even paying attention to the fact that they are free to leave now.

Oh, I get it, it was the first day and you have so much to tell your friends about and it is just burning your brain to have to wait and talk later. Sayyyyy, while you are home and on the phone maybe. Parents, you might as well just sit your asses out there in the heat and wait. These alien freshies are in no hurry to get into a car.

Handshakes, daps, hugs, and slaps on the backs and finally they seem to be heading to the door. Thank God. Hey you, what do you think you are doing over there. Get your lips off of that alien girl! Oh, I'm sorry. I thought you were an alien teen boy. Damn, it's getting hard to tell the girls from the boys these days.

Anyway young alien girl, you can't be kissing your alien girlfriend in the middle of the lobby. If the alien boys and girls are not allowed to do that, then you know you can't. sheesh! This girl-girl thing is wild. We will examine that a little bit later also. Just hang on, okay.

Nothing thrills a school faculty as much as seeing the school emptied of all of those alien teens. You can even hear yourself think again. The faculty understands that this is just the first day of many to come. Those freshie alien things will be right back here again tomorrow. I really don't think they pay any of us enough to have to deal with these off world characters.

Parents you must understand, no we don't love your alien teens like you do. We never will. They are rude, crude, disrespectful, hateful, and not to mention stink like a collard green fart. They are truly your problem.

We will do our jobs that we are paid to do. We will try our best to educate your alien teen and see that they have some understanding of how life works. The rest is really up to you. I pray your real teen will be released from that other planet and brought back home before this alien teen you are trying to rear, bites your head off and eats your guts. Alien freshies, gotta' love 'em…..Not!

Chapter 2

Girl's Outfit Switching Games

"Tonya, it's time for you to get on the bus. Don't be late. Momma has to get to work early. Come here and let me look at you. That looks really nice dear."

"Thanks mom. You better get going so you won't be late."

"I'm leaving right now. Don't forget to lock the door. Matter of fact, you need to leave now also. Grab your book bag and let's go. Honestly, I don't understand why you have to bring all those books home each day. I don't think I could lift that book bag of yours."

"heh, heh, heh. It's not that heavy mom. You really like these pants and the sweater?"

"Why yes. They go well together. You look just like a teacher yourself. Professional looking. That's my young lady."

"Okay mom, there's the bus. Gotta' run. See you when I get home later. Bye."

"Bye Baby."

Tonya is safely on the bus and with a puff of smoke, they are on the way to school. I think that was a rather nice conversation between mother and daughter. Does it happen like this in your house. Be honest. I know it varies from home to home, but it is mostly the same. Parents working hard to make a living and ensuring that their children have an easier life then they did.

That would be a great thought if you had your real child still in the house instead of that Alien teen daughter. Man the likeness is amazing. Remember, I was also fooled into thinking that my daughter was the real thing also.

The bus ride takes about 30 or 40 minutes at most. The first bell doesn't ring until 8:25 a.m. That is really a warning bell that another bell is going to ring. After all this time, no one really knows why you need a warning bell to let you know that another bell is going to ring. Who are we to question the school district, right?

The teachers are all present and standing in their assigned areas. The hallways are off limits until the 8:35 bell rings to head to class. In high school, your first class starts at the beginning of the day. You only go to homeroom during 3rd period. Even I thought that was strange.

Here comes Tonya's bus at the back of the building. I and Mr. Meene are always standing just outside the back door to greet the student aliens getting off of the bus. Not only that, we are looking to make sure that no one is wearing gang member bandanas, color doo rags on their heads, belt chains dangling from their jeans, afro picks with the metal teeth, and shirt tails hanging out. That's a biggie. School policy states no wearing your shirt tail out or your pants below your ass. They have to be up to your natural waistline.

We are really get tired of looking at boy "cracks" and funny color boxer shorts sticking out above their pants. You know that this fashion trend started in the prison system.

That's right. If you were available that night to give up some ass, you would wear your pants hanging below your butt. The prisoner who was going to get that ass would usually provide the lubricant. Sometime it was bacon grease. Whatever work or gets you through the night.

You try to tell these alien teen boys about this and they don't believe you. This "sagging" your pants fashion is the "in" thing. I have to admit, I tried it myself just to see what it was like. Suffice to say, this brotha' got too much "back" for it to work.

On the alien teen girl side of the house, we are looking for boobs popping out of tops, mini skirts that show your thong with each step. See through tops, too much flesh showing, hair wraps, and hair scarves. Believe me, we see and sometimes catch it all.

The alien students are pretty good natured about it and sometimes pretend they did remember they had a doo rag on. It becomes somewhat of a game of "gotcha."

Look at that parent of these alien teens. Did you see where all of those alien girls just went to? Straight through the door, bust a left turn and went right into the bathroom. Now you are about to learn one of the secrets of the alien teen girl race.

I'm standing just inside of the lobby now because I know what is about to happen and I want to bare witness. I, myself, am not the fashion police and take nothing to do with correcting what the aliens wear. That's the school's job. And they are welcome to it.

There must be 15 to 24 girls stacked up inside of the girl's restroom. It's almost like the circus clown car trick. How do they

They get all of those clowns in that little Volkswagen bug. Anyway, there they are, so many of them that you can actually see them jockeying for a space in the mirror or at the sink. They are applying make-up, doing each others hair, comparing notes about how beautiful or fine each other look. It is a frenzy of activity and a director could not choreograph it any better.

Okay, the face paint is on and the hair is now in place alone with the lipstick. Hmm, looking good alien girls. Here they come out of the restroom in pairs. But hold the phone, there is something else that has happened while they were in the "beauty shop."

I could have sworn Tonya was wearing a black pair of jeans and a matching black and grey sweater with sneakers when she got off of the bus. Her hair was up in a ball, held in place by some nylon wrapping material.

Parents, take a good look at these alien teen girls as they exit the restroom. Tonya is now wearing some "Daisy" duke short shorts, yellow in color. Her little brown ass cheeks are actually peeking out from under the leg with each step she takes. You can actually see that she is wearing a red thong right through the material of the shorts. Her top is a short sleeve shirt, low cut in the front. If I didn't know any better, she took off her bra. Her "girls" are hanging a little lower and bouncing a lot more then when she first got off of the bus. Topping this picture off, she has on some 4 inch high yellow pumps. We might call them stilettos if they were on the right person. Look at that, you can even see that she has a tattoo on her lower back where her shorts ride low. Looks like some kinda of Chinese symbols. Her lipstick is on very thick and her lips look a lot bigger than before.

I don't quite know what she is ready for, but it ain't just sitting in a classroom all day for 8 hours. Where is assistant principal, I. Hateeverthing? She is never around when you need the fashion police.

Look at the other alien teen girls filing out of the restroom. There are dresses so tight, you see panty lines too clearly. The ones you don't see must have taken their underwear off completely. There are the alien teen girls with the big boobs and too small bras, the shirts with the complete back cut out, more 4 inch heels and even less dress covering too much ass.

The alien guys are all in the lobby watching the parade of Hoes, I mean, alien teen girls prance around and looking sensual. Parents, it's so funny to see the alien girls holding on to each other so they don't fall off of those high heels. Before the end of the first period, you best believe they will be walking in bare feet from the pain. How d**o you alien teen girls squish your toes inside those too small size shoes. It's all for the sake of looking good.**

Alien teen girls do all of these things to entice the alien teen boys. They don't really want them physically, they just want them to admire them from a far. They want the alien boys to stand there and rub the front of their pants as they give them hardons. That's the name of the game parents. Make the alien boys get a woody, and you are one caliente mama.....

Parent's, when was the last time you looked inside those monstrously big book bags your alien daughters are lugging on their backs? Admit it. You stopped doing that when she started middle school. She needed her own space, and you had to respect that. But look at your alien teen now, half naked and giving alien boys woodys.

I don't think that this is what you had in mind when you wanted to show your alien teen daughter that you trusted her and respected her right to privacy. Sometime you just have to go back to those sneaky ways you use to have when you were being nosy. Go ahead and peek inside of those book bags when the alien is not looking.

What's she going to do to you, eat your head off and spit out the hairs. So tell me, who is the parent in this household? It's certainly not dad. Dads hate to fool with these girly type problems and are not well equipped to handle the fact that his alien daughter is showing off her boobies that you help make.

What's a parent to do? Be a parent, that's what. Pry, look, inspect and remind your alien daughter that while she is living under your roof, you are the Lord and Master of the Crib. Sure your alien daughter will spit fire and brimstone, but it will pass.

I'm kinda' joking here, but you should put your foot down when it comes to your alien daughter being well respected or sought after because she might be "putting out." Which is worst? Don't be afraid to pop up at school and have a surprise lunch with your alien daughter. The look on her face when she sees you will be "priceless." You keep a straight face though, and have a camera handy, 'cause she did the outfit switch game on you. You will want to have a Kodak moment when you catch her playing the game on you.

Just remember, you can't kill her and she's too big to stuff her back where she came from. Deal with it.

Chapter 3

Nut Check !!

Parents, lets talk about one of the stupidest games your alien teen daughters are playing all across the USA. As we know, alien teen girls are powered by thoughts of boys, boys and more boys. They want to know how they think, what they think, and what they look like naked. Oh come on, you know you did to when you were a teen mom.

I see them huddled together talking and catching a glance at some of the alien boys as them are standing near them. When the alien boy walks by, they hesitate until they can get a good shot at the butt in them jeans. Then they giggle about how tight it looks.

Some of the alien teen girls are a little more bolder then those wussies standing there checking out boy butt. They like to make a game out of stalking their prey.

The nut check game is mostly played by freshie teen alien girls. The upper classmen alien girls have probably gotten the opportunity to see the "goods" up close and personal.

For alien freshie girls, imagining what an alien boy's wiener looks like and how big it is, is of great fascination to them. Oh sure they have taken a peek at the playgirl magazine at the corner pantry or see a brief frontal nudity role in a movie, but it's just not the same as real life.

I don't quite know who came up with the idea of the nut check game, but they are one sick puppy. I had the opportunity to be in the right place at the wrong time to witness how the game is played. Check this out parent of these alien teen girls.

There are the alien girls standing over there scheming and talking quietly. They have identified their prey. It just happened to be a black kid named Travis. He was just leisurely walking down the hallway towards the alien teen girls. One alien girl broke loose from the pack and started walking towards the unsuspecting Travis.

Soon as the two got within arms reach, the alien girl reach out and grabbed the front of Travis' crotch area. She then yelled out, "nut check!" She gave is nuts a big squeeze and then let go. Travis curled up like someone had just kicked him in the nuts. I guess the alien girl squeezed his "boys" a little too hard.

All Travis could squeal was, "girl!" It was in a high pitch voice, just like a little girl's voice. The others in the group of alien teen girls were laughing their asses off. The alien girl that did the nut check on Travis turned around to her friend and held up her thumb and index finger. She was signifying that Travis had small nuts and a little dick. Her fingers were about three inches apart. Wow, that is a small one.

There were other alien boys and girls walking by and they were all laughing and pointing at the nut check victim. Hm, three inches. I would have to leave this area quickly as possible if I was Travis.

I really should chastise the alien girl for doing what she had just done, but it was just too funny. You have to have a good sense of humor when you deal with alien teens. Hey, it's the "nut check" game.

Chapter 4

Pantsed

I got to hand it to these alien teens. They can come up with some of the craziest things to get themselves suspended over. They never really escape that middle school mentality even though they are now high schoolers.

It's a nice sunny morning and the gym teacher has decided to take her gym class outside to the soccer/football field so they can run or walk around the track. That's a great idea. It gets the alien teen outside where they can do no harm to anybody.

The class is going well and there are no incidents or problems, or so it seems. Over there parents, see that group of three alien girls whispering and laughing as they walk behind Larry. It does not take much to guess that they are up to no good. I think I will remain right here and see what is about to happen.

I was thinking that they planned to slap him in the back of the head and run like hell. You know, the old game of chase me. I never get tired of that game myself. Seems like they have finally made their minds up as to who will do the deed and take the punishment is need be.

Alien teen Brittnay, a rather short, thickly built 10th grader was chosen to carry out the attack on Larry. She sped up to just behind him and keeps pace for a short distance. This was just like watching the wild kingdom, the leopard pacing the antelope. Waiting to bring the animal down with one mighty paw strike.

The other alien friends ran to catch up with alien Brittnay and her prey. With a quick look over her shoulder to her friends, Brittnay acted. The funny thing was, she didn't slap Larry in the back of the head, and she reached out and grabbed the bottom of his gym shorts and tugged them down to his ankles.

Larry tripped and fell forward with his feet tangled up in his gym shorts. He squealed like a little girl also as tried to pull his shorts back up. The alien girls were laughing really hard when they saw the little hole in the ass of his drawers. It was right where the crack of his ass was, as if he farted and "burned" a hole in his undies.

Then the chase part of the game started. For a large, thick, alien girls, Brittnay could run pretty fast. Finally at almost a complete lap around the track, he caught her. He tried his best to "pants" her, but the combination of her thickness and a tightly tied draw string kept him from pulling her pants down.

The gym teacher yelled at them to stop the playing around before they both end up in in-school suspension. She was not playing either. Larry stopped and Brittnay rushed back to her alien friends who were still laughing and pointing at him.

I knew alien Larry was not finished with that group of monsters. There is no way he would suffer that humiliation and not get a little revenge before gym class was over.

Sure enough, here alien Larry comes. He's running up from behind the alien group of girls and they don't realize he is there. He's running kind of on his toes as if he is tipping quietly upon them. This is gonna be wild when he finally catches up to them.

There was a fairly large group of alien teen walking just behind Alien Brittnay and her friends.

This was going to be a ready made audience if alien Larry is successful as attempting to do what he had planned. What that was, I don't have the foggiest idea. I thought he would maybe slap all of them in the back of the heads and then haul ass down the track. He had already attempted to "pants" alien Brittnay and failed. He can't be dumb enough to try it again and suffer the wraith of the gym teacher. Or is he?

Alien Larry is right up behind the alien girls and he's ducking slight down as if ready to strike. Then it happens. He reaches up from his slightly bent position and grabbed the bottom legs of the gym shorts of Brittnay's two alien friends and tugged downward hard as he could.

Down went the alien girls shorts to their ankles and they did not react instantly. They kind of froze in place with their shorts at their ankles and stared at each other in amazement and shock. This was too cruel. One alien girl was standing there frozen in her little dirty white, twisted thongs.

The other alien girl's ass was exposed because when alien Larry yanked her shorts down, they pulled her panties almost down with them. Her little ashy booty was exposed for all of the alien gym students to see and laugh their asses off about. Finally, they grabbed their shorts and rushed away from the track back towards the building, cursing all the way.

Unfortunately, the gym teacher witnessed the whole thing and of course alien Larry was suspended and sent to the school district hearing board for sexual assault. Man, tough break alien Larry.

What happened to Larry at the hearing board? He was a good student otherwise and because the alien girls pantsed him first, they had mercy on him and brought him back to school on probation.

Chapter 5

Horseplay gone wrong

Keep in mind parent's of these alien teens, sometime even having a good time with friends can sometimes take a turn for the worst. I know, your child/alien would not do anything that might turn out dangerous. You have taught them to behave in the school setting and to represent the family name well.

Ha. How wrong your thinking is when it comes to your alien teen. Take for example, just the other day in boys gym class, everyone was having a good time playing badminton, throwing the old football around and just sitting and chatting.

For some reasons, there are always those alien boys who don't like to participate in any of the sporting events going on. They would rather fool around and create mischief.

They love to horseplay around and just disrupt the class. The gym teacher, I'm sure, was getting fed up with having to yell at those two assholes that kept running around the gym throwing things at each other. The must have had ants in their pants, because they would not sit down for anything.

Alien teen Barry was a really stupid kind of a kid. The kind that you think might have been dropped on his head when he was born. Alien teen Chad was a really nice kid, but loved to play too much. Alien Chad, in his playful mood grabbed alien Barry's book bag and tried to run with it. The bag ripped and all of alien Barry's stuff fell out onto the gym floor as alien Chad ran away giggling.

Alien Barry was pissed. He picked up the first thing he could get his hands on and threw it at alien Chad, who was about 10 feet away. Just as Alien Chad turned his head to see where his friend was, boom! Alien Chad got hit right in the middle of his forehead by a large flying, math calculator. Ouch, that's gonna leave a mark.

The calculator exploded into pieces upon impact with alien Chad's head. You could hear the impact throughout the gym. It got my attention as well as the gym teachers.

Then the unthinkable happened. Alien Chad came walking over to where the coach and I were standing. He was bleeding from where the forehead. When I say bleeding, I mean his head was spurting like a fountain. It seemed that with each beat of his heart, blood spurted out in a long stream. Damn, he must have a ruptured artery in his forehead. The coach and I went into action quickly and grabbed him and some towels for compression. I got on my radio walkie talkie and called for an ambulance. The athletic trainer was summoned and he was shocked to see alien Chad spurting blood all over the place.

We got him into the training room and laid him down and tried to stop that damn bleeding. The white towels soaked red with blood as fast as we could change them. Where is that damn ambulance!

The principal was alerted as well as the school nurse. We had dreaded calling alien Chad's mom, but she needed to know. Here is the ambulance now. Alien Chad is loosing consciousness, but the trainer tries to keep him awake. He wants to sleep, but we know better then to let him.

Alien Barry was almost in tears from fear and sadness. He knew his ass was in big trouble when we finished dealing with this situation. The EMS workers got alien Chad into the ambulance and left for the hospital, lights and sirens blaring.

What the hell is that noise? Alien Barry is involved in a fight with alien Anthony, alien Chad's brother. Other alien students grabbed alien Anthony and I took him away and talked some sense into him. I didn't want his to get his butt suspended over what was a dumb horseplay accident. He calmed his jets down.

Of course the gym teacher was in a little hot water for not having control of his class thereby causing this tragic accident. Alien Barry was suspended and sent to the school district hearing board for causing another alien student's injury.

The parent of alien Chad came back to the school and really raised holy hell about her son's injury. It seems that the calculator struck alien Chad in just the right way to fracture his skull in the front. It also ruptured an artery which causes him to loose a lot of blood. He now has a metal plate in the front of his skull where the fracture took place.

Alien teens and their damn horseplay. No matter how much we as school administrators try to tell these alien students about the dangers, they still go out and almost kill each other in the name of fun.

Honestly parents, don't you think your real teens would follow your advice and not do such a stupid thing as I just described. I believe your real teens would heed our warnings. Too bad we are stuck with these alien teens until our "real" teen return from wherever.

Chapter 6

Food Court, that's cafeteria to you

Parents, the most favorite time of day at your local high school is lunch time. It's a time when alien students can unwind and take a break from the ho hum ramblings of a teacher whose trying to keep their attention for an hour. It's a time when you can hook up with your friends and compare notes, talk sports, girls, and cars. Sometimes not in that order.

This school has so many alien students that the lunch periods are broken up into 2 separate lunches. In the first period which last a mere 30 minutes, you have mostly the alien freshies and a few of the other grades sprinkled among them.

The assistant principal is always stationed at the door of the food court to make sure that shirts are tucked in and school id cards are being worn around their necks. It's also a good time to catch fashion no-no's on the alien girls. Dr. I. Hateeverything is really good at what she does. I love here to death. She even admitted to me that she is just a plain old redneck woman taking care of her elderly momma. That southern drawl of hers is priceless. In the beginning, I wasn't sure I would like her or if she would work well with a black guy comfortably. I was pleasantly surprised. She was down to earth, good people and would through her arms around me in greeting with not problem and always would come to my office to ask my advice on legal matters. We grew very close and I love this woman to death.

Back to the food court. You old parents use to go to a cafeteria in your old school days. When you were there, you actually ate the food and cleared your table, then went back to class.

Times have changed now that this place is inhabited by alien teens. They come into the court in droves making all kinds of noise. They are pushing and shoving and knocking tables to the side. They act as if they are starving, but alien teens only eat one kind of food, pizza. Make that two kinds of foods, burgers.

Most of the alien teens don't eat and use this time to hang outside the school building talking with friends. They are everywhere you look. We try to keep them all within eye range, but that is a lost cause. There are just too many of them to keep track of.

In the court, you can't hear yourself think it's so noisy. On the patio, some of the brotha's are in a big group doing "Rap Battles." My redneck alien students are in another group by the sidewalk talking about how much mud they got on their trucks over the weekend. The alien girls just talk to be talking. I don't think they even listen to each other, cause they are all talking at the same time.

Only the junior and senior alien teens are allowed to leave campus and go up to the nearby town of anywhere, SC to hit the local fast food joints. The security guard is by the parking lot to make sure each driver has a senior or junior id card. Freshies and sophomores alien teens can't go anywhere during lunch, they are not responsible enough.

There's Ms. Gotcha, an assistant administrator hanging out with the security guard also checking Id cards just in case he misses one. Lord, this little woman is good at what she does. We need more like her in high school. Plus the students are down with her also.

When the bell rings, it's time for the first lunch period to end and the next to begin. This food court will have less aliens in it 'cause most of the upper class aliens are in it. Most of them will drive away from campus and they think food court food is yucky anyway. I have always found it to be edible, but I'm not an alien, except to my ex-wife.

The best thing about the food court is that it gives us a little bit of a breather also. We actually get a chance to sit down and eat as well as chat with the alien teen about the latest happenings.

The alien teen really like the fact that I can talk their language. I can also dance as well as they do. I talk the same talk, alien-ize, and understand what makes them tick. They respond to me so well because they understand that I am not here to arrest them, but to make sure they don't get themselves arrested over stupid things when in school or in the neighborhood. It works out just fine.

Will you look at this? Parents please tell me that you did not leave you work place, drove all the way across town to bring your little alien teen some Mickey D's. You gotta' be kidding me. They could have walked their asses through the wood and got it in 10 minutes. Really, you have got to stop spoiling your alien teen this way or you will never get your real teen back. This one will decide to stay with you forever.

Enough said.

Chapter 7

Girl Fight!

Parents let's talk about a subject that affects just about all of us as parents throughout these United States. That subject is how we try to protect our alien teen daughters from other alien girls that want to kick their asses.

I know you wish you could be with your alien child 24 hours a day and protect them from any and everything bad, but we can't be there like that. We don't want to loose our homes to foreclosure or have our cars repo-ed. Not me.

When you send your alien teen girl to anywhere high school, you are entrusting the school administrators with their safety. Believe me, we don't want anything to happen to your alien child either. We kinda' like them, not much, but a little.

That's why we talk to them about right and wrong and threaten those who might want to harm your alien child over stupid things such as boys. That's right, I said boys.

Parents, do you realize that 90% of the fights we have in school between alien girls are over a boy that neither on can really say, they have legal papers to or the title on him? It is a fact. I see it too many times a year, we all do. You just had no idea that that's what's going down with your precious alien daughter.

Alien Girl fights are worst then alien boy fights. Alien boys will stand face to face and dare each other to take the first hit, hit me! No, you hit me first! I swear to God, I witnessed what I thought was going to be a fight in the hallway one day during lunch time.

They threw down their book bag, that's the sign for "it's on." Then they walk up close to each other, almost as if they were going to kiss one another. Here comes the threats and then the "I'm gonna' kick your ass" part of the prefight build up. They stood there for almost 4 minutes, wanting to fight, but not wanting to fight. They Desperately hope some of the alien students standing around waiting for the fight to happen, to pull them apart. That way they don't lose face or reveal the fact that they didn't want to fight in the first place.

Finally, I got bored and intervened taking one of the alien teens away. When the law takes you away by the arm, that makes you seem like you are a bad man that the law had to get you. Silly alien teen boys. You could almost see both of them breathe a sigh of relief that they don't have to go through with the fight.

Alien teen girls are a different matter. They are more dangerous then alien boys. If they say they are going to fight, you better get you ass over there quickly cause that's a safe bet. Case in point.

Alien Sonya had gotten herself pregnant by her alien boyfriend, Tray. She and alien Tray had been dating since the 11th grade. They actually broke up for a month over some nonsense that I can't remember. Alien Tray didn't want to be a daddy and made that clear to alien Sonya when they got back back together. She got the baby aborted for the love of her alien man.

Of course alien Sonya's alien girlfriends came to her a few weeks later and revealed to her that her boyfriend, alien Tray had gotten her arch enemy, alien Faith pregnant when they were separated. Oh you know where this is going, don't you.

What made matters even worse, alien Tray wanted alien Faith to have this alien baby. The alien newspapers were all over this news. The alien grapevine was buzzing hot with this news.

Alien Sonya was absolutely pissed! How could alien Tray talk her into getting rid of their alien child and then allow alien Faith to go ahead and have "their" baby.

Alien teen girls are so stupid when it comes to how alien teen boys think. We as grown folks know that men get over relationships a lot faster then women do. Women tend to love very hard, but guys will treat the break up like changing a flat tire. They put on a new tire and keep on going as if nothing had ever happened. Must be a nature thing.

Parents, here is the other thing that alien teen girls have in common with regular women. When alien Sonya got the news from her busy-body alien girlfriends, she immediately went on the "hunt." Not for alien Tray to kick his ass, but to find alien Faith, to kick her ass.

Now I ask you, who is the real guilty party here? Alien Tray or alien Faith. Male parents will tell you that alien Tray is the responsible one in this mix. Women will say that alien Faith is the problem, she did alien Sonya's alien boyfriend. But weren't they separated at the time? Women tend to forget that fact, don't they guys.

Alien Faith was coming down the hallway from lunch just as alien Sonya turned the corner near the wall lockers.

"Hey Bitch, how the hell you can be pregnant for my boyfriend, Tray?" roared alien Sonya.

"Bitch, you didn't want him, so I took him and we are gonna be parent to our little baby. You need to step off!"

"You red ass Bitch! You knew he was my boyfriend and that we were just having problems. You knew I was pregnant for him."

"But you ain't pregnant now, Cow!" oh, that one had to hurt.

At that point, alien Faith found her face meeting the door of the wall locker, assisted by alien Sonya who had her by the hair. It was on! Books were dropped and the two alien girls were swinging and punching for all they were worth. Alien Sonya who had alien Faith by about 60 lbs was laying the smack down on alien faith.

Just like all girl fight parents, alien Sonya who had the upper hand in this fight began to tear alien Faith clothes off. She actually ripped her blouse almost off of her body and was now hanging onto her bra cup. They slammed back and forth against the wall and the lockers. Alien faith was trying in vain to grab alien Sonya's shirt but couldn't handle alien Sonya's rage and strength.

They fell to the floor and alien Faith was completely topless with alien Sonya almost sitting on her boobs punching her in the pretty face. Alien Faith was bleeding from the mouth and her right eye was swelling quickly. Alien Sonya was merciless in handing out this ass whipping.

None of the alien students standing around the fight made any attempts to stop the beating. I don't know if it was for fear of alien Sonya's wraith, or they just wanted to see a good old ass kicking which is few and far between in high schools nowadays.

Just before word got to the administrators and teachers could get to the fight area, alien Sonya got up from her beaten prey. She hurled a few more words at her and then began to walk away from her laying there on the floor trying to cover up her breasts with her hands. Stupid alien students wouldn't even try to help her up or find her torn blouse to cover her.

Fortunately alien Sonya took a little pity on her and called off the beating when there was no fight left in her. She was crying at the thought of having destroyed her baby for her alien man and here is this other alien girl having alien Tray's offspring for him. She really felt the fool now.

Alien Tray was brought into my office and I spoke to him about the situation he caused. He said that he didn't want to be stuck to alien Sonya by an unwanted alien baby. He really liked alien Faith better cause she was so "fine." Alien Tray had no morals at all, like most alien boys with a hardon.

Alien Sonya, who is a junior, got suspended from school and sent to the school district hearing board. She was assigned to alternative school for 6 months, but could return to regular school with good behavior on her part.

Alien Faith lost her alien baby through a miscarriage. It was due to the terrible beating she suffered that day in the hallway. Her mother was kind of relieved that she lost the baby. She didn't like that alien Tray kid anyway and definitely didn't want him around her alien child because of an unwanted alien baby.

At last word, alien Tray is now dating a former friend of alien Faith. Former friends, because alien Faith found out that the former alien friend is pregnant by alien Tray. Man that alien boy gets around.

Parents, if you take one thing away from this incident, teach your alien teen about the perils of thinking you have found true love in high school. It's just being horny that is getting mixed up with feelings of love.

I know, I know, they are not going to listen to you and your advice, but you have to put it out there. Don't be afraid to talk about sex to your alien daughters and sons. If you don't, they will learn about it from their alien friends at school. Then you will catch hell from the mess that will be created by your not doing the right thing.

You should not be ashamed to talk sex with your alien teens. The fact that they know you know, will cause them to think before they do anything stupid. It's not going to work all of the time, but your mind will rest better knowing that you did a parents duty and put it out there.

Also remember, I know you told you alien teen that if someone hit you, you better hit them back or you will hit them when they get home. All parents say these things. Admit it.

If an alien teen fights in school, it don't matter who started the fight, they both are going to get suspended. No ifs, ands, or buts about it. That's policy. Alien teens know if they have a problem with another alien teen. They need to let us know before it turns into a fight where they both will lose. Remember that and don't get mad when the principal suspend your child for "defending" themselves. It doesn't work that way anymore. I know that's bad English, but efficient.

Chapter 8

Diss 'da Teacher

The one thing that really pisses me off is the lack of respect your alien teens show to the teachers. It's been said that the hardest job in the world is teaching somebody's alien child. It is a thankless job at best. Low paying and filled with long hours and much stress.

Alien teens have no idea how hard it is to be stuck inside of 4 walls each day for over 250 days a year for sometimes 20 or 25 years. When you think about it, the only thing a veteran teacher of 25 years has to look forward to is dying and being buried and forgotten.

Alien teens always blame the teacher for anything that doesn't go their way academically. They don't really look in the mirror and see where the real problem lies, you are a dummy and that's why you failed!

Teachers are some of the most dedicated people on the planet. I had the opportunity to become a teacher, but turned it down because I like being able to run free and be outdoors. Teachers don't have that luxury. They have to use their every free moment to teach hard headed alien teens and when not teaching, they plan the next days teaching lessons. It's a vicious cycle isn't it?

But you know, know matter how hard the great people work to get your alien teen to the end of the road to graduation, they are dissed by the alien teens as well as you parents. Oh yes, I have been there when you come into the school blowing flames from your noses because your alien teen secretly phoned you and said they were being done wrong and picked on.

You parents take the bait and without even getting the other side of the story, the teacher's side, you are ready to kick their asses or go to the district office on them and try to screw up their jobs. You need to quit this stupidity. Honestly, it does not make you look like the most intelligent person on the planet. It makes you look and act like an alien teen yourself.

Parent's, do you know that your alien teen tell lies? Huh? Not my alien teen. They would never lie to me, their parent. Ha, ha, ha, have they got you fooled. I sit back and watch how these alien teen actually have you "trained" to respond to their every call and hang on their every word as if it is a true fact. Bow your head, you know it's true parents.

They say the nut don't fall far from the tree. The way you parents act is the same way your alien teen act. We see it constantly. Sometimes we have to wonder who the boss in that house is. Most of the time, it's the precious alien teen who is running things, you just don't know it.

Parents of alien teens, get a hold of yourself and use common sense the next time your alien teen calls you and tells you the teacher is picking on them. Out of 2,400 alien students, what makes your alien teen special enough to pick on. Think bout that when that call comes.

If you want to break your alien teens hold over your mind and body, the next time that calls comes, ignore it. If they tell you're the teacher is holding them hostage against their will, tell them, "that's nice, have fun."

Teachers are your best friend's parents. Who else will voluntary babysit your badass alien teen 9 hours a day for you, for free? Who?

Chapter 9

PDA (Public Display of Affection)

The really fun part of being a high schooler is that you get to do a lot of cool kissing. Man these alien teens love to press the lips together a lot around. I wish I had stock in the lip balm market, I would make a killing the way these aliens suck face.

Don't be surprised, you sucked a little face in school also. I know I did. That's why I'm an expert face sucker now thanks to Arlene during our junior year. Kissing her was as far as she would let me go. I never did make it to home plate with her. Oh well, her loss.

As soon as alien teen walk through the doors in the morning, the daily ritual of kissing starts. Most of them know that the school forbids the open display of affection, but hell, when has that ever stopped an alien teen from doing it anyway.

You have your "before class start smooch." Your "glad to see you at lunch kiss." Your "thanks for walking me to class smack." Your "nobody's looking quick lip lock." Then there's your see you back in school tomorrow good-bye kiss of the day.

The next day, we start all over again with the kiss ritual. Oh I almost forgotten, your hanging out in the parking lot suck your lips off kiss. Theses are almost X-rated. Gotta' love these school cameras.

The teachers are usually pretty good at catching the violators. The good thing about it for the alien teen is they catch them after the lip lock has happened. So they win. You need ESP to know when these kisses are about to happen.

The best method to try to prevent the kiss from happening is to talk to them during orientations at the beginning of school. The only alien teens that really abide by the no kissing rule are mostly the alien teen freshies who aren't getting any, anyway. Who wants to kiss them?

The other punishment if caught 100 times is in school suspension. That's a small price to pay for a good lip slob. Don't you think? The main reason for the no PDA is to try and instill a little respectability to each individual. Mostly the alien females.

Why do you ask is it mostly aimed at the alien females instead of the alien guys? There is a very simple answer to that question. Let me put it to you this way.

You are an alien girl and every time your fellow alien students see you, you are lip locked with somebody. Several times a day, throughout the day. You know alien girls are cruel people and they are going to start labeling you as a slut, ho, trick, easy, bitch etc..

When alien boys are lip locked with several different alien girls each day, they get the label of; he's da man, Mr. hot stuff, got it goin' on, Big Daddy, etc..

Which label would you want for your alien teen. So watch out for the PDA and be careful how many times you might be kissing different alien friends each day. Oh and parents, if your alien daughter is wearing a collar shirt instead of her low-cut boob show-er, she's got hickies, she's got hickies. Some passionate little alien boy has sucked the hell out of her throat. He has marked his territory for all to see at school, but it's not for viewing by the parents of the alien girl. That marking might get him "terminated" by the Dad.

Chapter 10

High School Dances (Sex with your clothes on)

One of the most fun times in an alien teen's life is going to the high school dances. This is the chance for them to blow off some steam and sometime create more "steam."

The student activity director is always the one to coordinate any of the dances that the school wishes to throw for the alien students. School officials actually understand that all work and no play causes hell in the classroom if these aliens don't release that pent up energy.

They have valentines' day dances, fall dances, lunch time spirit week dances, prom dances and once in a while, fund raiser dances. It's the only time the alien students get to dress like they really want to. Either in some very "fly" clothes or jeans kinda' sagging a little. Of course the alien girls can let their boobies out for air also.

With all of the music and Rap stars making dance music these days, they have learned that to sell a lot of records, you have to make a dance hit. Whether it's "cranking dat superman", "Swag 'n Surf", or the "Booty Doo," I never tire of watching the alien teen do their thing on the dance floor. I also was down with the dance craze in my time and to today still can "drop it" like the best of them.

What get's the school teachers and faculty's dandruff up is the fact that the alien teen like to "body Rub." This is when a couple get together on a slow song and actually simulate having sex with their clothes on. No kidding, I'm a witness. It's the wildest thing you will ever witness your young alien teen doing.

The real movement of the dance is the alien boy will just stand there with his crotch thrusting forward, hands down by his sides. The alien girl will lean forward and back her ass up to his crotch. Then she rubs her booty up and down and around and around against him his crotch.

Some alien girls will do the "turk-ulator" or the "Booty vibrator" in conjunction with rubbing her ass against his crotch. I tell you, I have seen those same moves at the strip club and on the latest Rap videos. Some of your alien teen daughters are going to have a great future if they go into the strip club as a star.

The whole idea behind this dance for the alien girl is to get the alien boys dick hard and then to "ride" it. She thereby is in control of the mindless alien boys. All he can do is stand there and tremble and let his mind go to a "happy" place. It is too strange to watch.

The teachers and activity director catch hell trying to separate those locked together bodies. When they separate one couple, the other couple is back at it again. It seems like a lost cause to waste time trying to fight that dance style, but the teachers give it they're best effort on your behalf, parents.

There was actually one school district in the Atlanta, Ga. Area that cancelled the Prom because of all of the problems with this "nasty" dance the alien students persisted in doing at every sponsored dance they held. The parents put a lot of pressure on the principal to stop that "sex with their clothes on" style of dance their alien kids were doing.

News flash parents, it's not the principal's fault that that's the way your alien child is dancing. You need to take responsibility and talk to your little alien about respect and don't let the DJ play slow music. Enough said.

Chapter 11

Gangs 'n the games they play

One thing I have no time for alien teens playing the "gang" thing. These are the knuckleheads who are literally cavemen playing with fire. Like the caveman, they all will get burned.

Parents, the gang thing started back in 1972 in La. The Crips were the first known gang during that time period. They were simply a high school sports team of jocks. They basically bullied other kids that attended their school and harassed cross town rivals.

They adopted the color of blue to represent them, as is today. These aliens had no idea that a high school bit of nonsense would still be in force with us today.

Because of the invention of that gang, other gangs and groups began the same stupid voyage. Now today, we have several dominate groups of criminals running around all over America and even in some parts of the outside world doing it.

The average age of a present day gang member is 15 years old. I'm talking not just alien boys, but alien girls as well. They mostly come from low income families where the Dad is missing in action. The mom works probably 2 or 3 different jobs to make ends meet. These young aliens don't have much and they are given the opportunity to "get" more then they have. That's how it begins.

Here in school and as well as in the local neighborhoods, we have 3 dominate gang groups, Crips, Folks, and the largest one, the Bloods.

The Crips are the smallest of the 3 and use the color blue to represent themselves. They have sometimes run hand in hand with the Folks in different neighborhood. We really don't see too many of these aliens around any more in SC. We all know the most famous Crip member of all is Snoop Dogg. He made it popular and it still is today, but over on the left coast...that California for you laymen.

The Folk Nation are the guys in black. They identify themselves with everything worn to the left. They place their black bandana in the left hip pocket if you get a chance to see one live and in person. They also use the 6 pointed star of David to represent themselves as well as a 3 point pitchfork pointing downward. Crazy, huh?

Then there's the People Nations, better known as the Bloods or the guys in red. This is the largest of the 3 criminal groups. They identify themselves with the 5 point star, carry red bandanas in their right pocket, and use the 3 point pitchfork pointing up as a symbol.

These three alien groups all hate each other and have killed so many of each other over things like neighborhood owning, disrespecting each other, jumping each others members when they see them, as well as fighting over which businesses they want to rob.

The bottom line is that these aliens carry guns and are very dangerous. A lot of you parents have these aliens living in your house and you either have your head up your ass, or you are ignorant as hell. If you really know your alien child, then you will know when something has changed about him or her. But you don't ask them questions, do you?

You will be amazed at how many times you parent find out that you have had an alien gang member in you house when it is to late. Once again, I have to ask you, who is the boss in your house, huh?

Ask yourself these questions and at the end, you will know whether or not you are literally living with an alien gang member.

1. Have you noticed a change in your alien teen's attitude.
2. Does your alien teen not want to go to school at all.
3. Does your alien teen wear a lot of red or black clothing.
4. Does your alien teen have clothing that you didn't buy.
5. Does your alien teen have money all of the time, but no job.
6. Does your alien teen have bad grades, discipline problem.
7. Does your alien teen hang out with aliens you don't know.
8. Does your alien teen hang out late or is mysterious acting.

If you take the time to pay close attention to your alien teen and find that he is exhibiting several of these telltale signs, then you need to act as soon as possible.

Go to school and check out his grades, talk to his counselor, check with the SRO at the school. Ask him to show you his my-space or face book webpage. If they refuse, then who pays the bill here? Insist on it parents, don't be a pussy when it comes to finding out about your alien teens possible gang involvement.

Once an alien teen is in the gang, he is "down 4 life." This mean the only way out of the gang is to die. Once a gang member, always a gang member. That is the motto of these twisted alien kids. The bad thing about it is that you parents don't make the time to talk to your alien teens or get involved with what they do at home and in school.

How do they get into the gang? What causes an alien teen to want to join? What do they do once they are in the gang?

Let's take a look at those questions. There are 3 ways to get into an alien gang;

1. Jumped in (as many as 10 alien teen beat the hell out of you for 35 seconds and you have to stand and take it.
2. Blessed in (your immediate family members are in the gang so you are given a "pass" to join. They simply punch you in the chest one time. You are in.
3. Sexed in (this is for alien girls. They have to have sex with all of the alien guys present. Usually without a condoms).

Some wannbee gangs who are not true gangs will allow you to get out of the alien gang by the same method you got into the gang. Real gang members are in till they die or get killed.

The average age of the gang members we have found killed or murdered has been 15 years of age. That includes alien boys and girls. So you see that it is very important that you truly learn about that warm body that is living in your house eating your groceries.

There are wannabe alien gang members in every high school and neighborhood in America. You must be vigilant and teach your alien to know better.

Spend time with your alien teen, do fun things together, go to church, get them involved in sports and clubs at school, and take him to sporting events and vacations. Show a real interest in your alien and you will make it hard for those so-called alien gang members to recruit your flesh and blood. Remember to keep your alien safe.

Chapter 12

Drugs…Hook a brotha' up

The high school officials and the district office have made it their priority to call a war on drugs in school and on school grounds. I commend them for their effort. After all, it's hard enough for the teachers to pour knowledge into these alien teen's mind without drugs interfering with the process.

Drugs are in all schools. Some alien teens are a little smarter then others when it comes to hiding it from the faculties attention. Most of the time, they will get "snitched" on by their fellow alien students. That's the one thing we as lawmen can count on when it comes to good alien teens, they don't want this filth in their nice school.

Parents, if you are doing drugs yourself, how the hell can you tell your alien teen not to do what your are doing. That's the stupidest thing I have ever heard. Do as I say, not as I do. Most of the times, the alien teens we catch comes from homes that "don't" do drugs. That's a good thing.

Alien teen smuggle their marijuana into school in the first place I will look, their book bags and their underwear. You are fooling yourself alien teen if you think I won't stick my hand into your drawers and pull out that bag of weed. I'm pulling the first thing I get my hand on, nothing personal, just business.

And you parents are so offended and hurt when you have to come to the school and see your alien child sitting in my office with his hands cuffed behind his back and tears in his or her eyes. I feel bad for you parents. Sometimes you can do the best you can, but you have to realize that there are forces in school much stronger than your parental influences.

I tell parents often, never say what your alien child will not do. You don't know their social habits once they are away from you and meet up with their alien friends here at school. They are Jekyll and Hyde personalities when they are here. That's why you need to make it a point to come and visit your alien child in school. Show them that you care.

The drug situation nowadays is not half as bad as it was just 5 years ago. More and more alien students are using good common sense and understand that drugs are a nowhere trip. But don't think it still won't happen to you and your family.

Getting caught with drugs on campus is an automatic suspension and trip to the hearing board. That's just like going to court at the school district. It's not a pleasant place to go. On top of that, I'm going to charge and arrest you. You will wear the silver bracelets. If you are 16 or under, you get to go home with your mommy and she will bring you to your court date. If you are 17 or older, so sorry but you are gonna' take that long ride down the street to the brick house with barb wire around it. You did the crime, now you're gonna' do the time.

Let's hope your alien kids make the right choices when they are confronted by a stupid alien that tries to get them to try it.

Chapter 13

Morning restroom trips

As I said earlier in this book, alien teens have a strange need to go straight to the bathroom when they get off of the bus. I think it might be because their houses don't come equipped with toilets and sinks. Then again, some alien teens might like to have an audience around them while they are making number 2 in the stall. Splash, splash!

At anytime during the morning, there can be over twenty something bodies hold up inside the alien girls and boys restroom. They are definitely not resting in there. The alien teen girls are pretending that their restroom is a beauty shop / changing room. On the alien boy's side of the house, their restroom is used to primp and look at themselves in the mirrors under restroom lights. They are worst then the alien girls.

There use to be a problem that when you see a large group of alien boys or alien girls pile up inside the restrooms, there was going to be a fight. If it was not a fight, then they were doing gang stupidity such as initiations and meetings.

Thanks to the sharp eyes of the faculty and me, we have a pretty good handle on the restroom situation. I could care less if the alien girls come out of the restroom wearing only G-strings and a smile. It's the alien boys that concern me more. Their minds are so weak when it comes to being suckered into becoming gang members.

There are cameras and eyes everywhere, so they behave. To clear the restroom quickly, simply ask the alien teen boys if they are checking each other's dick sizes out, and watch 'em run out quickly!

Chapter 14

Rappin in 'da boyz restroom

Parents your alien teen boys are in that damn restroom every morning they come to school. What is the interest in such a smelly place when you have such a beautiful almost new school to hang out in? They are primping in the mirror and looking at themselves like the alien girls, but these alien boys are doing something extraordinary. You might even say it is very talented what they're doing.

When the music field of Rap came into existence, it took the world by storm. Even country music stars use Rappers in their lyrics. Alien teen boys are also on board with doing the Rap thing. They have even taken it to another level with "Rap Battles."

"Rap Battles" are alien teen boys who freestyle their lyrics as opposed to reciting a written rap song. They make the words up right from the top of their heads and spit it out without stopping or pausing to think of what to say next. This takes skillz and a quick wit.

I walked in on a battle in progress and sometimes when one participant is getting his ass kicked, they want to fight. It doesn't happen often though. If you can't quick rhyme, don't put yourself out there to get beat up and laughed at.

This particular morning, they were kind of loud with all of the laughing and yelling. Someone was getting his tail handed to him during the battle. I think I might want to take a peek in on this one just in case it gets a little out of hand. The principal had no problem with the alien students horning their skills because it really takes a lot of talent to do this type of Rap.

I walked into the restroom and there must have been 20 alien teens in there surrounding the two who were Rappin' against each other. Alien

Todd was basically tearing up alien Wilbert with a quick and rather nasty worded Rap. I have to admit, his flow was pretty good even though it was kind of spotty at best.

Alien Wilbert tried for a comeback, but the crowd was clearly on the side of alien Todd. When you got the crowd, you got the battle won.

Alien Wilbert stopped abruptly, out of ammunition and stuck. He had lost and the crowd cheered alien Todd. Then alien Todd made a stupid mistake and called me out. "Come on Dep, I'm right here, you ready for this ass whipping?" Oh no he didn't. I told him, one shot, winner take all, you go first.

He laid down his rap and it was weak as pond water. Only a few little parts flowed but it was not his best. Kinda' hard to "do" a Deputy in your rap battle. My turn. You know I kick it ol' skool flavor...

You flunked everything in school, except PE
You as dumb as a rock can be. You wear nice clothes, pockets really Phat. You always walk with boys, where the hell your girlfriend at. Oh I get it, you must be gay, is that the reason you walk that way. Yo hair look nice, your booty's looking fat, come on guys, you really wanna hit that! I think you lost, I see through you just like glass, now all you guys get your butts to class. Now wave to Todd cause he's looking really gay, Come on now Todd let me hear you say it... Heyyyy!

Chapter 15

Girl – Girl luv is 'n da air

You know parents, jut when you think you have seen everything, something comes along and replace the last event. This next chapter is just one of those head shaking, roll your eyes up kind of happening. I should be use to the fact that alien teen girls are always doing things we least expect. It's in their nature.

One of the special times of year around a high school is Valentines Day. The week leading up to that special day always create a buzz in the air about who is going out with whom.

This time of year, those alien girls who want to get an alien boys attention is now bold enough to ask if they like them and want to date them. I can't believe how bold these alien girls have gotten. In my time, it was the boy that made the first move and then if that didn't work, we made like Keith sweat and begged like a dog.

Everywhere I look, the alien teens are carrying heart shaped boxes of candy a balloons that are almost bigger than they are. It's a great sight to see. For a school of almost 2,400 alien students, everyone is being nice to each other. It's so cool to witness.

The alien teen throw the no kissing rule out of the window when they walk their sweeties to their classes. I really don't try to get involved with that type of thing. It's more of a school rule and not a law.

Oh my God, there goes alien Kathy, the top basketball player on the girl's varsity team. She is holding hands with alien Latonya, a cheerleader.

What the hell is going on here?. There they go, down the hallway, alien Latonya with an arm full of teddy bear and smiling her butt off. I think I need to go that way and check the classes which were changing.

They got to Ms. Alston's math class and stopped to chat a little. With a last smile at each other and a big hug, they then lip locked each other. It was a long passionate kiss and the other alien students passing by barely noticed this.

They finally broke contact when the teacher approached and hastily split. This was an event that was playing itself out all over the school. Alien girls kissing alien girls. Didn't matter if they were black or white students, they were kissing their asses off. The rest of the population of alien students did not pay any attention to this girl-girl thing. Strange.

It's happening in every school in America, even in middle school, they are experimenting with gay relationships. You have to wonder my dear parents, where did you go wrong with this alien female. Is there something you could have done to prevent this and is it too late to make them like alien boys again.

Some of the alien girls were actually trying to look like alien boys. They wore only blue jeans and sagged their pants just like the alien boys do. Some had cut their hair short to look the part of the male partner when they were with their female friend. Some have gone so far as to wear too small sports bras to flatten their breast down so they look more masculine. I almost fell to the floor when I saw this one alien girl dressed like a guy and I could have sworn she had a penis. Could be a rolled up sock in her crotch area. That was too much.

I was chilling in the lobby one day when all of a sudden, a whole group of alien students started running out of the door and up towards to the end of the building near the patio area. I also ran in that direction. When you see alien students running, it means only one thing, a fight!

Once I got to the patio, which was in front of the gym, I saw a parent who had gotten out of her car and grabbed one of the fighters and was leading her away from the other alien girl. Another parent had jumped out of her car to help break up the fight. The assistant principal, Mr. Doorears appeared behind me as I arrived to take hold of the alien girl who was fighting.

The fight was between alien female basketball player Laura and alien female basketball player Karin. Also present and screaming at the top of her lungs was my little best friend alien Beverly, the cutest of the cheerleader at the school. I quieted her down and we all went to the assistant principal's office. I let Mr. Doorears handle his business as I was not going to press any charges for a simple fight with no injuries.

It not our job to give these young alien people criminal records at such an early age, so it's best to let the school handle it in-house. Also, we will need these two alien players for a big upcoming game in three weeks. You know that's how some schools handle their business. Quit playing like you didn't know parents.

It didn't take long to find out why the best two players on the girls basketball team were fighting each other. It had nothing to do with being fired up from basketball practice. This fight was because of love and wanting to be loved. Isn't that the way life is with humans.

As the two players told their side of the story, the school officials could only shake their heads and try to hide their disgust at this sordid story of why the two best players would risk everything and fight each other.

The fight was over alien Beverly. They both were so in love with that little alien girl. Truth be known, I had seen alien Beverly walking and talking with alien Karin sometimes and at other times, she was hanging around alien Laura's neck like a necklace. Sometimes I have seen alien Beverly kissing one, then she would appear at another part of the building kissing the other one. This was going to come to a head real soon. It did, and it caused a big disturbance.

Alien Beverly wanted to talk to me because she was upset about the whole situation. I told her that you knew this was going to happen sooner of later. If you want to be with one of them, chose the one you want to hang with. You can't have it both ways. She had a look of amazement in her face. As if to say, I want both of them.

What was even crazier is the fact that she had a real alien girlfriend that she has been dating for 2 years at our rival school across town. So why are you playing these two aliens girls. What is the reason for causing this mayhem. She said, "They are both good love makers." Wow, I would expect that answer from an alien boy, but not this petite little alien thing.

"Alien Beverly, how did you end up like this, I mean liking alien girls instead of alien boys."

She looked at me and settled in to explain the whole situation. Boy I wish I had not asked. But she was comfortable enough to explain the whole thing to me.

"Dep, it all started in the 7th grade, there was this girl who was a dyke, a male type girl. She really liked me and would always ask me if I wanted to get together with her sometimes. I would always tell her no and that I was not down like that. As time went by, she and I kind of became pretty good friends and even invited her to a sleep over at my home.

Once again, she asked me if I wanted to try it. She keep wanting me to let her eat my pussy. I was not going to let her do it, but I figured if I let her do it one time, then she would drop the subject. I was kind of like her only friend cause the other girls were scared of her. She did look like a boy.

That night she got in my bed and I let her eat me. Boy that felt so good and I almost screamed and woke up my momma. She was smiling at me and telling me that this is what I had been missing. Then she told me to do the same thing to her. I told her I didn't know how to do it, but she said she would teach me. I got between her legs and she was trembling and moaning and jerking just like I had done. That's when I knew I liked it. I like eating pussy and having mine eaten. Boys are afraid to do that to a girl."

Upon that note, alien Beverly, you need to take your butt to class. I had heard more than enough to last me a lifetime. Parents believe it or not, this same story is being played out throughout all of the middle and high schools.

These unsuspecting alien girls are convinced to do things such as this and then they are convinced that it is a natural thing. I don't know if there is an answer for you parents out there that are having the same issue with your alien daughter.

The best thing you can do is continue to love them and be there for them. They may change, they may not. My bet is on the "not."

Alien Beverly's mother came to my office one day and I asked her how she handles the fact that her alien daughter loves alien girls. She said that she tries not to think about that and just love her for who she is, her alien child.

The one thing she did say she hoped would happen is that she takes a alien boy to the prom and not an alien girl. I had to laugh along with her on that one. I even passed that wish along to alien Beverly in hopes that she would make her mom's dream come true.

She did just that. When alien Beverly got out of that stretch limo, she had an alien boy on her arm and looked like a walking, living dream. Alien teens clean up so nicely during prom time. They came into the prom room and took pictures and everything.

When the music started, all bets were off. Alien Beverly was once again hanging around alien Laura's neck like a necklace once more. Well she did carry out on the promise to arrive with an alien boy, but there was no mention about after they got inside.

Gotta love those alien girls who love alien girls, they are still ours to keep for now until our real teen come home.

Chapter 16

Tuck it in and hide the boobs

One thing I really love about high schools is the fact that they actually do fill in where you parents leave off when it comes to teaching your alien teens better manners. That's not to say that most of you out there don't to a hell of a job rearing your alien kids, but there are those of you who have been slacking off and letting your alien teen get away with murder when it comes to fashion and looking presentable.

Case in point, we really do have a fashion police in every school and it's a really dirty job filled with disrespect, dirty looks and sometimes back talk from the alien teen that was busted for a fashion faux pas.

The alien teens are checked out as soon as they get off of the bus or walk into the building from their parent's vehicles. Those parents in the vehicles have pretty good control over what their alien teen is wearing. Those on the bus get away with a lot of fashion mistakes.

The policy is pull your pants up to your natural waist line you alien teen boys. We do not want to see what color or style boxer shorts you have under your jeans. I'm still wondering, those alien boys that wear their pants down below their asses, how in the world do they stay right there and not slip down to your ankles.

It's the craziest thing. They actually keep the jeans from sliding down to their ankles by walking slightly wide legged or bow legged. That's got to be very uncomfortable, but they do it. Pull 'em up, now!

There is a "tuck" policy in effect also for the alien boys. This is a good policy because with the gang stupidity going on in many of the schools, you would be amazed at how many weapons one can hide under those over sized shirts. That's the other thing about this new fashion for the alien boys, everything they wear is 3 or 4 times larger then they would actually wear.

Alien boys are warned to tuck it in and pull it up. For the most part the will start tucking shirts in and pulling their pants up before they get to the building so we don't have to say anything.

Soon as they get around the corner or down the hallway out of sight, the shirt tails comes back out and the pants drop back down their backsides. It's almost like a game of "catch me if your can."

If they are caught, you end up getting in-school suspension or work detail after school. I think the punishment fits the crime. For the most part, you only see the black alien teen boys doing the sagging and bagging thing. They are so into copying what they see in music and rap videos. I think if a rap artist jumps out of a window, we would have to nail all of the school windows shut to stop them from following the trend.

Alien teen girls have a problem with trying to show all of their "goodies" to anyone who wants to see them. The fashion police is really effective in saving them from themselves. As I told you before parents, your alien daughter might have left home in jeans and a nice sweater, but once they made it to that alien girls restroom, they transform completely into a different fashion diva.

The mini skirts, the see through blouses, the really to short shorts, the 4 inch heels, the too short shirt that shows your have a tat across your lower back, or shows that you finally got that fly belly button ring in your navel. It's all about looking "hott" for the alien boys willing to look.

My dear parents, do you dress like this when you are going out with your girlfriends? Well I can't really blame you for this thing of showing what you got. It's the darn video vixens in the music videos that have started telling our alien children what trends to follow and how much of their bodies to show. It's not just teaching them the latest dance either.

Parents, take my advice, check those book bags. Make a plan to visit your alien teen during lunch. Hell, have lunch with them, they will enjoy it and it will give them a sense of dread that you may pop up and any moment. Pay attention to what your alien teen is wearing when they leave out of the door.

For you parents who leave home before your alien teen, you have but to give a quick call to your alien child's guidance counselor and ask them to check out your alien child. They will be glad that you are showing such interest in keeping them focused on academics and not chasing alien boys.

Come on Parents, help the school out in trying to keep your alien teens focused on what's really important, education.

Chapter 17

Special Ed Teens, Gotta luv 'em

One aspect of high school that really tugs at your heart strings are the mentally and physically handicapped alien teens the school is charged to educate.

One really never knows why the Lord chooses to bless certain families with a child that is not as "complete" as the other children that may be in the family, but nevertheless, you are the parent and must treat them with as much love and caring as you can muster.

All high schools are equipped to handle those special needs alien teens and they get that extra special attention necessary to keep them growing mentally.

My heart goes out to those teachers who have studied and trained to handle those special aliens' teens. I know I would not have the patience or the inclination to learn how to take care of special needs alien teens. Thank God there are great people, great teachers who care to go that extra mile and care for them.

Make no mistake about it. I have witnessed how caring these special teachers are. Sometimes, even they get a little angry when an alien teen acts out of character, but they are able to re-focus and do what necessary to straighten that alien teen out.

Yes, I know you hear tales and rumors of abuse of these mentally and physically handicapped alien teens. Believe it or not, the abuse is usually happening at the home and within the family that alien teen belongs to. Never have I had to investigate abuse of a special need alien teen in high school. Now ask me how many times I had to go to the home and investigate the parents. A totally, different story there. Particularly when the special needs alien teen tells us themselves what is happening at home.

Most of the time, the abuse happens out of frustration by the parent. Dealing with a "special needs" alien teen is one of the most mentally taxing jobs on the planet. We don't pile on top of the parent and try to cart them off to jail. Rather we get the department of social services to get involved and find a solution to help that frustrated parent. That's the best remedy.

After all, if we take the parent away from the alien teen, who else will have the patience and love to take care of him or her outside the family unit. No one.

That's why my heart goes out to alien foster kids around this area. Alien foster kids catch the most hell when they are misplaced into certain homes. I don't buy the excuse from the department of social services that they are doing the best that they can. Bull shit!

They are never around when you need them. They misplace alien kids in home without really taking the time to see if there is a good fit. And don't let there be "abuse" of an alien foster child, that's when they really work hard....to scam their way out of admitting they screwed up. I have witnessed it first hand. They need to get their "act" straight just as the DVM worked to get themselves after public attention caught them with their pants down. It shouldn't take an alien child getting hurt for these agencies to do their jobs. Enough said.

Chapter 18

I got a gun...and I will use it

It's a normal day in high school and all of the alien teens are in the respective classes. There are no aliens roaming the hallways or creating a disturbance. Darn, it's a really boring day. Well I can occupy my time with conversations with the various faculty or get ready to conduct some law related classes. The teachers love the break in the action when I take over their classes of alien teens.

Suddenly into the discipline office pops alien teen girl Ryann, and she's looking like she's seen a ghost. The discipline secretary intercepted her and questioned her as to why she is out of class. She barely paid any attention to the Secretary. She says she needs to see the Dep.

I beckon her to come in. Alien teen Ryann is one of my favorite alien students in that she and her sister sang in a talent show I sponsored for "special Olympics." She definitely was not here for a social visit.

The first words from her lips were, "Dep, alien Carl has a gun in class and he tried to make me put it in my book bag. I told him no!"

I sat straight up at those words. This is one of those things that we are actually placed in school to prevent. When you have a real life situation, you have to act as quickly as possible, but you mustn't attract too much attention and panic the whole school.

She told me which class she was in and that she told the teacher she had to go to the bathroom. She came straight to me. I asked her to tell me exactly where alien Carl was sitting and how many alien students were sitting near him. I had already formulated a plan. I contacted assistant principal, Mr. Cardoorears and he appeared almost like a genie into my office.

The plan is for alien Ryann to go back to her class and take her seat as usual. We would wait about 7 or 8 minutes and enter the class. Once inside the class, we would take all of the alien students sitting at that particular table and bring them back to my office, book bags and all.

The plan went very smoothly and we had 5 alien teens in our office. Mr. Cardoorears had all of the book bags. We split the alien teens up and the assistant principal began questioning one of the alien students in the office next to mine. I had an alien teen named Jose in my office along with alien student James.

As we sat there and they tried to bombard me with questions as to why they were there, I noticed that they were quite nervous. Especially alien teen Jose.

"Stand up son, I need to check you." My cop intuition was buzzing as hard as Spiderman's spidey senses when it warns him of danger.

Alien Jose stood up and I went quickly to his shirt, pulling it up and reaching my hand into the front of his pants. Bingo! A nice little Glock 40 caliber auto-pistol. Similar to those our female deputies use. Alien Jose's face went white and his knees went weak. I told him to sit down and alerted the assistant principal that I found the gun.

As I held the gun and threw questions at the alien suspect, he weakly managed to say that the gun was not his. Not his? He went on to explain that he was only hiding it for his alien friend James. Alien teen James just sat there and did not show any emotion or say anything. He was playing it "hard." I like when they play hardcore, makes it more fun when they break and start wanting to call their mommas.

I alerted my supervisors at the Sheriff's Department and he was on his way. My job was just beginning. I needed to know the rest of the story. I read the two alien teens there Miranda rights and they said they understood them. The assistant principal alerted both alien teens parents and they were on the way to the school.

Alien James was in a talkative mood finally. He had tears in his eyes as if he was remembering something horrible. In truth, he was.

He told us that he knew where his dad kept that pistol and he had planned to use it to kill his dad when he comes to the school to pick him up. This made our mouths drop to the floor. This young alien teen was deadly serious about his plan to murder his father. We needed to know what would motivate an alien teen to want to "off" his own flesh and blood, his father.

Come to find out, his father had been seriously "abusing" and beating his mother almost to the point of unconsciousness. He had also hurt his sister who required treatment at the emergency room just days earlier. I knew I had missed her from school for a few days. He went on to say that he was going to make him stop hurting his mother for good. His words were cold and emotionless.

The parents showed up and the story was related to them and there was a lot of emotion and electricity in that office. Even the news media had camped outside the school waiting for and exclusive on this story.

Here's the other crazy thing about this whole incident. When I pulled the pistol from the alien teen's pants, the first thing any good cop does is to check the magazine and see if it's loaded. The darn gun was empty!

When I pulled the empty clip from the weapon, alien teen James eyes grow large and his mouth dropped open. It was clear that he knew nothing about guns cause he was genuinely surprised to see that there were no bullets in the gun.

"Kinda' hard to kill a man with an empty gun, son."

You know it's ashamed that these kinds of things happen at home, but ultimately end up coming to school to play themselves out. Your local schools have been the place for many situations to act out. Some funny, some crazy, some very dangerous. Like this case.

What happened with this situation? Well the two alien teens were arrested and placed in juvenile jail. Alien Jose, for possession of a weapon on school grounds. Alien teen James, for possession and bringing a weapon on school grounds. Doesn't matter that it was not loaded, that's the law.

The best thing to come out of this is that the abusive father/husband was arrested and charged. The mother and her family were given the help they needed. Alien James was given the mental help he badly needed.

Chapter 19

Mickey D's at all costs!

Parents, one of the funniest things I enjoy about watching your alien teens frolic about the high school campus, is their love for McDonald's burgers and fries. The alien teens refer to this fast-food place as Mickey D's. That slang name has actually become the official name of the franchise and has sometimes been used in their commercials.

As you know, food court food sucks! So says the upper classmen aliens who have nice cars they can use to drive away from campus and hit the fast food joints.

It is the craziest thing to see when the lunch bell rings and they know they only have 30 minutes to get to the food joint, eat and get back before the end of lunch bell. They make it happen with no problems.

The freshie alien can only stand and watch and dream that one day, they too will be able to treat themselves to the Mickey D's trip. That brings to mind the main reason why we have the security guard and an administrator standing at the end of the parking lot checking id cards.

Think your alien teen is not desperate to taste the awesome grease and salt of those fries? Check this out.

One day, the security guard and an administrator were standing in their usual spots checking ids. The car full of alien seniors or juniors would speed away with not problems.

When you have studied the minds of the alien teen as I have, you understand that some things concerning them are not always what they seem.

It also helps to have a little birdie whisper in your ears sometimes when there are things we need to know is going to happen around the school.

Sometimes it a matter of safety and sometimes it just plain fun to thwart the things alien teen try to get into.

This day I decided to hang out with the security guard and the administrative assistant at the end of the parking lot. The alien teens were zooming by as they normally do. I was positioned on the opposite side of the road then the two school officials. I was paying close attention to the cars as they rolled up to show their Id's.

Hmmm, that one car seems particularly low in the back. I waved for the security guard to stop this one car. He did with a curious look on his face. The administrative assistant was curious about why I was stopping the flow of traffic wanting to leave campus for lunch.

"Hey there, teen alien senior. Open your trunk. No, don't stand there questioning and trying to act all innocent, open the trunk."

He did and what did we find? Two freshie alien teens were trying to sneak off campus to get to the glory land of Mikey D's.

"Get your asses out of the trunk and go back to the school. Now!"

They could not run fast enough to get away from us. As for the alien senior, who were smuggling illegal alien freshies, you loose your privileges to leave campus for one week. "Get to stepping back to school."

All for the love of a good Mikey D's burger and those delicious fries. Mmm!

Chapter 20

"Dep, I'm hungry

Another thing that sometime pulls at your heart strings parents is when an alien teen comes to school hungry. That is one of the most saddest things that can happen to even an alien teen.

Depending on where your high school is located, you will find that there are a lot of alien teen who actually come to school hungry. I don't mean your normal, you just woke up and you need to eat something. I mean alien teens that went to bed hungry and will be hungry until they make it to the food court the next day.

We are living through tough economic times and there are a lot of families out there in our communities who are barely earning enough to make ends meet and keep food on the table. It a "sad state of reality." Not everyone was born with that silver spoon in their mouths you hear speak of. They have to make do with the hand dealt to them.

I've had alien student ask me for change to buy chips from the vending machines because they are hungry and don't have any money. Their parents can't afford to pay for their lunch daily either. The school does a good job with the free lunch program. You would be amazed at how many alien students rely on that free lunch to get them through the day. Some will not eat again till lunch time the following day at school.

I commend all of the teachers who allow students to eat lunch on their lunch account. I also have fed the masses when they approach and ask. Sometimes I would see alien students who were too proud to even ask for food sitting there looking into space. I would offer, and most times they would accept. Makes my heart feels really good.

Chapter 21

You ain't takin' my fone

Thanks to good ol' captain Kirk and his star fleet handy dandy communicator, we now enjoy the same instant contact with whoever we chose to talk or listen to.

That same form of instant communications has been hell on the teachers in every high school in the country. Our alien teens have a great need to call each other and talk about fashion, where they will be going for the weekend, or did you see that alien boy booty at PE.

I have never seen alien people with the need to talk so much about not a damn thing. Sometimes they just stand there holding the cell phone to their alien ears, smiling at nothing. Amazing.

These darn cell phones you parents have bought your alien teen so you can keep in "contact" with them have cause a lot of problem for school administrators in high school. There are actually school policies to prevent alien students from using them right in the middle of a teacher trying to prep for an upcoming test.

Then there are the smart alien teens that use there cell phone to photograph the test and email it to their alien friends so they will have a leg up on scoring well. You have to admit, that's kind of smart for an alien teen.

Parents, you buy those darn things for your alien teen to keep in touch with you, but they use them for everything but call you. But oh let them get into trouble and then they will finally call you to try and get them out of the frying pan.

Cell phones are wondrous inventions when use for the right purpose. It is rarely that these alien teen know what a right purpose is. They take it upon themselves to think they can just walk down the hallways and talk as if they are on the sidewalk. How dare they.

Alien teens really don't like to talk into those futuristic pieces of plastics. They would rather send text messages instead. Plus, it's a lot easier and quieter to text to your alien friend while you are in class. The teacher won't know a thing. She is so busy trying to teach that she has no idea. You are talking to 200 aliens friends a minute.

Have you ever seen these alien teens work the text on those cell phones? I swear they can text a message almost as fast as I can say the words the old fashion way by talking. It's sometimes fun to watch their little alien fingers move at the speed of sound sending messages that don't mean anything. Wish I could do that.

Every now and then, an alien teen gets busted texting in class. The policy is that the alien must give up the phone. This is not an easy thing for an alien teen to part with half of their "brain." Taking that cell phone is like taking a baby from a mother, almost impossible. Believe me when I say that alien students would rather get suspended then to turn over to you their cell phones.

The get really nasty, they growl, and sometimes act as if they might bite you if you try to take it from them. That's when the teachers have to call the "heavy hitters" to go in and extract that precious piece of gold from a vicious alien teen.

They try to come up with all kinds of excuses as to why they can't turn over the phone to us. it belongs to momma, it's a friend's phone, and I need it to listen out for my dying great grand mother. We really don't care what kind of weak or lame ass excuse your alien teen wishes to offer up, give up the damn cell phone.

It's a darn shame that an alien student would chose to take a suspension rather then hand over the cell phone. This alien child has her priorities misplaced. Whoever the parent of this alien is need to get her home and beat that ass. ASAP.

If that's the way you want it, sweetheart. You are suspended until such time as you are willing to give the school the cell phone. Ah ha, you didn't see that one coming. They really mean it when they say you can stay home suspended until you hand over the phone. I don't think your parent will back you up on that decision.

Common sense finally kicks in and the alien teen turns over the cell phone. Now you are still going to get a couple of day in-school suspension and work detail for putting us through this who drawn out affair in the first place. You have just experienced what we call a lose situation. I'm so sorry.

That's a minor thing compared to the alien teen girls who take pictures of their private parts and email them to their so-called alien boyfriend. He in turn emailed the photos to all of his alien friends and now everyone knows all of your intimate secrets. Wow, someone is actually looking at your naked booty on the library computer. What a dummy.

Of course that alien teen's mother is having a stroke when she learns that her alien daughter is out there like a porn star. Leave it to and alien teen to take a great invention and turn it into a sideshow. Not to mention all of the harm it does when it is misused like this. Parents, get a handle on your alien teen as well as your phone plan.

The schools can only do just so much to try and regulate the use or misuse of cell phones on school grounds. They are at the mercy of the alien teens and the parents that give them the phones and forget to provide guidelines for the use of that wondrous communicator.

Chapter 22

Bus dat nut (Bus luv)

As you know, my dear parent's of alien teens, the one thing you can count on from your alien teen is the fact that they are sex driven. No matter where you turn in the high school, there is some form of sexual activity going on between alien boys and girls. The faculty does a good job of trying to identify and prevent it, but they can't be every where all the time.

Alien teen sex can happen in the blink of an eye, or the turning of a back. Then boon it happens and then it's done. We missed the whole event. Ah these alien teens are a crafty lot. There will be away to catch them one day in the near future, but right now it's a hit and miss game.

Alien teens use the school bus like we used our cars at the drive-ins. It a great time to fog up the windows while the movie previews are playing. You break contact the minute the real story starts. We had a system at those good old drive-ins.

The school bus left the school as it does every day on it's appointed route to take these alien's home after a full day of learning. This was not going to be your ordinary kind of bus ride, not today.

Alien teens Jordan and Anna were sitting on the front seat of the bus just behind and to the right of the driver. They were involved in a serious conversation which ended with alien teen Anna nodding her head yes. She reached down and picked up her book bag from the floor and placed it between herself and alien Jordan who was next to the window.

Alien Jordan leaned back in the seat as if to get comfortable. He then unzipped his pants and took out his penis. Alien teen Anna kinda' looked at it and giggled a little. Keep in mind that this is a bus load of

62

alien teens laughing, talking and playing around as the bus went down the highway.

Alien Anna then reach over and grabbed alien Jordan's penis and started to jerk it up and down. She was moving her hand up and down really fast as alien Jordan laid there making faces as he enjoyed this little sexual play.

The bus driver, for some reason, glances back over her shoulder in the direction of alien Anna just for a second as if she knows what was going on between them. Alien Anna stopped what she was doing momentarily until the driver stopped looking.

The driver looked back towards the road and alien Anna started her rapid pace jerking of alien Jordan's body part. She was working hard and fast. She even stopped and adjusted the book bag so it hid what was going on from the driver.

Alien Anna was getting tired and leaned forward for a minute. Probably wondering what was taking alien Jordan so long to orgasm. She sat back upright and as she watched, alien Jordan finally released his load all over her hand. She then reached into her book bag, got a tissue and cleaned her hand as well as alien Jordan's private area. She took the tissue and stuck it back into her book bag just in time to get off at her stop.

This whole incident was recorded on the bus video cam and the driver was livid that this took place right under her nose. You can't really blame the bus driver when you are dealing with these crafty alien teens. It could have happened to anyone.

Chapter 23

Discipline office regulars

In every high school, you have what's called your disciplinary office. Within those walls you will find an assistant principal, a discipline secretary, a guidance counselor and the school resource office. It's a pretty well run operation if I do say so my self.

The best thing an alien teen can do for themselves is to stay far away from his office. There are hundreds of alien teens running around this school who I will never know their names. I will see them and remember them by face, but by name is asking too much. The fact that I don't know them is a good thing. If your butts been in the discipline office, you bests believe I know your name, address, and your parents names.

Of almost 2,400 alien teens running around this beautiful building there are only about 100 aliens that will be known to us by name. that's not good. It means that you are one of the regulars of the discipline office. You are the alien teen that has caused your mom to have to leave work and drive 500 miles to come and pick your sorry behind up because you have been suspended again.

And Parents, don't play us that it's our fault that we are always picking on your alien child and that he can't breath without us harassing his alien ass. You should be ashamed of yourself for even thinking of such a thing. With over two thousand aliens running around, what makes your alien teen special enough to require our special attention. The answer: your alien child is BAD!

He's all yours to do with what you so chose. Make him clean the house and then go clean the neighbor's house next.

Chapter 24

Janitor's Nightmare

Janitors in high schools are the hardest working people in the whole building. You thought it was the teachers? Come on now, give the Devil his due. These guys and girls have the ungodly job of picking up and cleaning up after some of the nastiest alien teens to walk this planet. They do it with pride and are commended for jobs well done. The pay definitely does not match the effort these great people give.

The bad thing is when one bad apple is laying in wait among the good apples. Parents, that bad apple really can spoil the whole bunch if you leave it in the basket long enough.

For almost a month I and the assistant principal had alien teen boys coming to our offices complaining of having money stolen from their wall lockers. There were wallets being taken, pants being searched through and replaced and gold chains and Ipods coming up missing. It was enough to drive us crazy. We had to do something about this mini crime wave.

We checked the wall lockers and found that they had not been pried open and the locks didn't seem to be tampered with either. This was really perplexing and the parents of these alien boys were beginning to breathe down our necks for answers.

All of the keys to these wall lockers are held only by the administrators and the coaches. We figured that there must be some knucklehead teen alien boy who had gotten his hands on one of those keys. The problem is, there are hundreds of aliens in the building and they are not just going to turn themselves in.

The plan was put together and laid out that we would plan to be in the area of the locker room around the time that the thefts normally took place. It seemed that the first lunch period was the prime time for crime in the locker room. That gave myself and the assistant principal a starting point to try and solve this crime of convenience.

We sat in the head coach's office, which was like a fish bowl because of the way it was designed with all of that glass. The lights were off and the office was pit black. We sat back and waited patiently. We could see clearly down the rows of the locker as the lights were on as usual.

Then it happened, that darn assistant principal reached over and touched my ear causing me to almost jump through the glass thinking that a spider had crawled on my ear. I could have kicked his ass for that prank, but he knows that this means war after we catch the locker room bandit. Big dummy!

Within minutes, our wait was almost over. Someone had just walked into the locker room and was walking up and down the rows of lockers. When we could finally see who it was, the head janitor, we relaxed again as he always checks the locker rooms and assigns the other janitorial workers the job of cleaning up if the place needed it.

What the hell? All of a sudden, the head janitor looked around and then took out his key and opened a locker. He took out a wallet and then emptied it of some money, then put everything back into place. Damn!

We sure as hell did not see that one coming. We waited until he finished his searches. He must have gone into 7 or 8 lockers removing cash and a couple of times, an electronic device.

As soon as he was done looting the lockers he began his long walk back toward the door area. Soon as he got only several steps from the door of the locker room, the assistant principal turned the lights of the coaches' office on. At the same time, I step outside of the office and in between the door and the head janitor.

I half expected him to do something stupid like run or take a swing at me and bum rush through the door to freedom. He did neither. He simply dropped his head and shook it from side to side in a apologetic fashion. That was all well and good, but it did not change the fact that he had just committed a crime and for that, I had to take him into custody.

I escorted him to the main office and the principal came in and did his thing. He called the company manager for which the janitors work for and who assigns them to each school. Needless to say, the manager was not a happy camper and said do what you want to do, the head janitor's fired. Just like that.

As much as I hated to do this to the head janitor, the law is the law. We had shared some great times and good conversations over the years we were assigned at this school. To think that after being sports buddies for several years, now I would be prosecuting him for larceny was never in the cards.

The ride was long and very quiet. I turned on the local talk radio station to break up the long dead silence. It took my mind off of the fact that this guy, this friend, this criminal had ruin what started out to be a good day.

Chapter 25

Locker room orgy

As we discussed previously in a former chapter parents, your alien teen are solely motivated by sex. With it being all around them in the movies, on the park bench and even at the beach, it's no wonder their little motors are always revving to go.

I was walking around the school building as I normally do, just checking for anything that might be out of place. Sometimes I may walk up on an alien teen cutting class or aliens hiding out in the parking lot because they hate going to Ms. Smith's math class. If there is anything out of place, I will find it.

Hold the phone, what do we have here. The alien boy's locker room's rear door has been propped open with a rock. That is not normal. I backed away from the door and called Mr. Doorlikeears to come and meet me outside of the locker room. As soon as he arrived, he and I walked quickly into the locker room with the element of surprise on our side.

In the locker room were 5 alien teen boys and 1 alien teen girl. The alien girl was leaning forward with her hands resting on a bench and was wearing no pants or panties. There was an alien teen boy behind her that was about to do the "nasty" with her. The other alien teen boys all froze in place with a look of fear that was almost comical.

The alien girl tried to hide her shame and tried to find her pants to cover up. We turned to give her a as much privacy as possible while keeping a sharp eye on these alien teen boys.

All of the aliens were escorted to the discipline office and we got to the bottom of what we had just witnessed. The alien girl was just sitting there expressionless. She did not even flinch when the assistant principal told her that her mom was on the way to the school. There is clearly more to this alien girl than meets the eye.

As for the alien boys, four of them admitted to all agreeing to go into the locker room and have some fun with the alien girl. She had actually agreed to go into the locker room and play nasty with them. Talking to the weakest link of the alien boys, he informed us that while in the locker room, the alien girl had given them all blow jobs just before we bust into the room.

The other alien boy was not going to be satisfied with a simple BJ, he wanted to "stick" something. She agreed to let him do it. Wow, these alien teens are something else. If we hadn't been there ourselves, we would not have believed this story.

All of the parents came and picked up their alien teen boys who were now suspended for sexual activity on school property. They all would have to go to the hearing board for such a serious infraction. As for the alien girl, her mom explained to us that she was her foster child and that she had been taken from her regular home a few years ago because she had been raped for years by her step father.

I knew there was something seriously wrong with this alien girl. She was still acting out because of the traumatic and criminal acts she had to suffer for all of those years. She acts out sexually and cannot control it. This is not the first time I have come in contact with alien foster kids who were mentally damaged by their own parents and they have no way to defend themselves. It's a sad state of affairs.

All of the alien boys were sent to an alternative school where they would have to stay until they prove they had learned their lesson about doing such a stupid thing as they did in the locker room. The parents were really pissed that "their" alien teen boys actually did something so crazy at school. A few of the parents could not wait to get their alien outside before they gave them the old back handed slap besides the head. Those are so priceless. We don't call that abuse, we call that parenting.

The alien boy who was so anxious to "stick" something ran into me down town at the mall a few days later. He was really embarrassed to look up and see me standing there. I chatted with him for a little while and he began to feel a little more comfortable around me.

Before I left him, I told him that he was one lucky alien guy. The fact that we rushed into the locker room saved him from having a really bad school year. He looked puzzled as I began to explain what I meant by that statement. I went ahead and broke it down so he would understand a little better.

"Alien son, if you had gotten the chance to "stick" that alien girl, you would be at the clinic with an STD."

His mouth dropped to the floor and his eyes were big as saucers. That's right, the alien girl had the "clap" and you would have had the drips had we not barged it and stopped you. This was one of those Kodak moments. He looked like he didn't know whether to shake my hand or kiss me. Alien teen boys, gotta' love em.

Chapter 26

Stairwell BJ

Here we go again. I'm telling your parents, you really need to have "the talk" with your alien teen about sex. Between two caring people, preferably adults, it can be a wonderful and fulfilling thing. In the hands of alien teens, it becomes something you witness on a porn video. It's like arming a child with a Glock 40 auto-pistol and telling him to go and play in the streets with it. It's crazy.

It was another normal day in alien land and all of the population was tucked away in their respective classes. I and the assistant principal were sitting in my office joking with each other about who we thought was hot among the substitute teachers. Come on, you know how we men think parents. Ask your husbands. On second thought don't as him anything. He still has to live with you for a long time.

The janitor came into my office in a frantic way and told us that we are not gonna' believe what she just saw. You know we love a good mystery. So we listened to her story and then we hurriedly made our way to where the situation was happening.

As we got down to the third stairwell area of the school, we slowed our pace to a slow tip. The janitor told us to take a peek into the open area which housed the staircase. She said to look at the glass doors that lead to the outside and we will see what has disturbed her so.

We both leaned around the corner of the door well and looked straight ahead into the glass doors leading to the outside. In the glass we could see a reflection. It was two alien students behind the staircase itself.

What we witnessed was simply amazing and to be honest with you, really stupid. We could see the reflection of an alien teen girl on her knees in from of an alien teen boy who had his pants down around his ankles. The alien girl was actually giving the alien boy a BJ right in front of a glass door.

Oh man, we have to interrupt this right now. We burst into the staircase area and quickly appeared to the side of the stairs where the two aliens could see us. There was a flurry of movement from the teen aliens as the alien boy tried to pull his pants up quickly as possible. The alien girl jumped to her feet wiping her mouth on her dress sleeve.

Now you know there are no words that can explain what the hell we just witnessed right here in the stair well. The alien teens did not even offer up any kind of weak explanation at all. They simply bowed nothing that I could really say either.

That was a long slow walk to the office. I'm sure the alien teens were trying to get their stories together in their own minds. They don't realize that the picture says more then their words will ever say.

The assistant principal called the parents and once again they were on the way to an unknown situation with their alien teens. The policy dictates that we don't discuss the whys over the phone. Just get your parent ass here as fast as possible. Parents, when you are making that drive to the unknown, you should prepare your common sense mind. Don't start girding yourself for battle with us.

Both parents showed up at the same time and walked with each other down to the office where we were waiting to deliver the bad news to them. This part of an administrator's job is always the hardest thing that he has to do. They are not here to hurt your parent feelings, but he is obligated to tell you the whole truth about your alien teen, no matter how harsh or disgusting it turns out to be.

Telling a mother that her alien daughter was in the stairwell, on her knees, with a strange alien boy's penis in her mouth is not a pretty thing to have to deliver. The mother was torn between crying, screaming, or ripping her alien daughter's head off of her neck. Fortunately I was present and she knew that I would not allow her to commit murder right in front of me. She'll do it later at home where there are no witnesses.

The alien boy's mother basically just sat there and looked at her alien son and just shook her head. She mumbled to her alien son that he was a "dirty bastard" just like your dad. Wow, I did not see that one coming. I think she was referring to the nut not falling far from the oak tree. Her icy stare was enough to drop the temperature of my office a few degrees. Otherwise, she maintained her composure.

I couldn't believe that the alien girl gave the lame excuse that she gave him a BJ because he wanted to fuck, but she wasn't ready for that. Wow again, I didn't see that one coming either.

Talk about your twisted frame of mind. Parents, do yourselves a favor, don't hesitate to have that "talk" and keep talking. I know that with some alien teens, they will probably still do the nasty, but your mind will be better able to heal when your are blindsided like this.

A little prevention, is worth that pound of cure. Enough said.

Chapter 27

Parent's vs Teachers

One of my favorite subject's parents is the day to day problems that occur when your alien teen has a conflict with their teacher. This is something that happens probably dozens of times a day in every high school you have ever been in.

Parents when you guys are going to realize, teachers do not have time to "pick" only on your alien teen. There are thousands of other aliens running around the different classes that they have to contend with. They really don't have the time to single your alien out to give him or her hell.

Alien's teens are notorious for not following the school rules. When they get busted they want to "buck up" at the teacher and try to make the teacher fear them. Or they try to intimidate the teacher into backing down from them. Wrong answer Parents.

I see it time and time again. Little alien Johnny once again is caught skipping class and the administrator is obligated to call you and let you know that he is being given a suspension.

Before he can get off of the phone, you are rushing through the door and demanding to talk to that dirty low down administrator who's picking on your alien teen. You don't care that you are making a spectacle of yourself in front of the nearby alien students in the lobby. Other parents are turning to see who that crazy person is creating such a disturbance in the middle of the school.

Irate parents never really take the time to realize that your are making an ass of yourself you wonder why we have so much trouble with your alien teen. Remember that nut that doesn't fall far from the tree? This is a prime example. Someone needs to hold up a mirror to that parent so she can see herself at this very moment.

Once in the office, you barely let the assistant principal get the explanation out as to what the problem is before you are interrupting his and trying to tell us that "my alien Johnny wouldn't do such a thing." Got news for you, thats' why his ass is here now, he did do it.

It's always funny to note a parent's reaction to my entering the office when things start getting a little loud between you and the assistant principal. I enter the room in hopes that my presence will calm your temper down.

On the contrary, you parent's look at me and sometimes actually tell me that you "ain't" scared of no police. "If I need to tell you off or curse you out assistant principal, then I'm going to do it. Cop in here or no cop in here."

"Oh hell to the No!" let me explain to your Ms. Parent of an alien teen, "If I feel that you are totally out of control and are to threatening to the assistant principal, then I will either escort you and your alien teen off of school property or charge your with breach of peace." That will take at least $300 of your Christmas money from you for being so rude.

We really don't need to go there alien teen parents. The best method is to calmly listen to the explanation of what your alien teen did and also give him time to explain how he can actually help the situation. Kicking your alien out is the worst case scenario. Work with your school administrator and you both will come to a happy medium.

Chapter 28

"You fucked a white girl?"

Here comes an alien teen girl into my office and she is in tears and can barely form words. I go into my investigatory mode and set about trying to find out what had caused this alien to shed so much water from her alien eyes.

The assistant principal joins me and we begin the process of trying to extract information from this alien girl in order to help her. She finally calmed down and looked us in the eyes and said that she had just been raped.

That word made everyone in the office go silent. You could have heard a pin drop when she laid that information on us. We go the nearest female guidance counselor to join us and that is the school policy. And the assistant principal began his questioning. I listened intently.

She told us of how she was walking down the upstairs hallway with a teen alien boy named Eric. She said they were talking and laughing about different things including sex. They made their way down the hallway and were near the lockers and the restrooms. Alien Eric said that he needed to use the restroom and wanted her to wait on him.

She stood by the outside edge of the restroom door and without warning. Alien Eric grabbed her by the arm and started trying to pull her into the alien boy's restroom.

She tried to struggle and get away but he was too strong and kept saying that this is what they wanted to do. Let's not just talk about it, let's be about it.

With that she was finally pulled into the restroom. Once inside she related to us that he held her with one hand and pulled her pants and underwear down with the other. He also dropped his jean to his ankles.

Once that was accomplished, he pulled her into a stall where he set down on the commode and pulled her down on top of him, forcing her to engage in sexual relations.

She told of how painful the act was and that she began bleeding. Even though she was crying and telling him to stop. He did not hear her. She said he finally loosened his grip on her and she jumped up, pulled her clothes up and ran out of the restroom, leaving his there.

That sure sounds like rape to us. The alien girl's parents were contacted as well as the alien boys. Another administrator located alien Eric and brought him to the office, but out of sight of the alien girl. We did not want to traumatize her any further.

I have been a cop for a long time and can usually tell when I'm being sold old used swamp land by a crook realtor. Something about this didn't feel right. My spider senses were tingling very badly.

I told the assistant principal, who was ready to crucify the alien boy for doing such a heinous crime in his pretty school, to hold the phone and let's give the alien teen boy his day in court. We need to hear his side of the story. I used that word very lightly. He was sitting in the connecting office and had a look of "what did I do?"

I told the alien boy that his friend had accused him of raping her. He almost jumped straight up from his chair and hit the ceiling. He was frantic and pacing and saying such things as, I don't believe this, she's lying, and it was her idea to have sex in the restroom. He wanted so desperately for us to believe him. He was tearing up and his voice was cracking very badly.

He almost had a total melt down when told of the punishment for such a crime in the school and what the law would do to him for the rest of his life. Rape can carry confinement of up to his 21st birthday or beyond depending on the Judge.

He was really crying a river now. I pulled the assistant principal to the side and told him that I believe this alien boy. He's telling the truth. What he did was plain dumb and stupid, but he's truthful. On the other hand, our alien girl is the worst liar I have seen in a long time.

Did I mention that the alien girl was white and the alien boy was black? If I forgot to mention that, now you know. They were both 15 years old and in the 10th grade. From what I knew of them, they both were B students and had no discipline records at all since being in this school. Once again, that demon called sex has created mayhem.

The alien boy's dad showed up. He was estranged from the alien boy's mother, but the mother could not get away from work due to their strict policy there. The dad was irate and loud talking and letting the alien boy have it with both barrels.

He was almost in tears himself from anger after I told him the penalty for rape. That set him off even more. He paced up and down my office wall. The principal had joined us and wanted to tell the dad the school positions concerning this bad situation. The dad threw up his hand and raised his voice to heaven again. He was being very dramatic if I do say so myself.

The alien boy was really crying and looking at me pleadingly. There was nothing I could do for him. He may have done the crime and will do the time if prosecuted.

What was a highlight in this room full of emotion was the day asking the alien boy who what that little alien girl you had in the bathroom. Is she from our neighborhood or the neighborhood a few streets over from us? They lived in a mostly black neighborhood in their town.

The alien boy looked at dad and said, "No dad, she don't live anywhere near us. She's white."

When the alien boy said those words, she's white, the dad grabbed his heart, then his head and looked to the heavens again and yelled out, "Oh God, you done fucked a white girl? Oh lord Jesus, please help us!"

I and the principal quickly exited the office and stood in the hallway bent over laughing our asses off. What the dad had just said made it sound like his alien son was gonna be hanged for such a crime as "doing" a white alien girl.

This really made me understand how backwards some people really are when it comes to racial stereotypes. I imagined the dad thought the Klan would ride into the school at any moment and take his alien son out to the fields. That was so stupid. You had to be there.

To make a long story short, as I said, I did not believe the alien girl's story from the start. I was correct in my investigatory knowledge. Here's the real deal or story for the unhip as born out by our good old school video camera system. Love those cameras.

On video you could see the two aliens walking down the hallway and they did stop at the restroom. The alien boy went part of the way in and turned to the alien girl as if to say, "you coming?"

The alien girl looked all around and made sure no one was coming or in the area. Then she rushed into the alien boy's restroom voluntarily. Yes they did do the "wild thing." What turned this little sexual liaison into something scary was the fact that the alien girl was a virgin. During the act, she started bleeding and it scared the hell out of her.

She did not know what to do or how to handle the fact that was caught off guard by what is actually natural for the first time. Her biggest fear was how to tell her mom the reason for her clothing being bloodied. That fear of mom made her take the "low" road. She lied and cried "rape."

She didn't think or care that she was about to ruin her former alien boy friends life, she just wanted to protect herself. A very sad state of affair. I could have stacked legal charges up against her for lying and filing a false police report. As well as lying to the school

Officials. We are not here to try and cut a young life short before it has a chance to blossom. All alien teens will make mistakes, some of them worst then others, but you still want to help that alien person all you can.

They both were suspended from school and sent to the alternative school. Both were remanded to the sheriff's department youth program which is serving probation and work release for a determined period of time. It's better than going to juvenile jail.

Parents, this was one time that the curiosity about sex that teens have could have resulted in a young alien boy's life being ruined forever. We cannot neglect our duties as parents to talk to our aliens about doing the right thing. Telling the truth is easy, it's lying that can result in someone truly being hurt, arrested, or even killed.

Sometimes the truth hurts, but there is no substitute for it. Relay that along to your alien teens when you get the opportunity to do so. Remember, you are the parent, the boss. Your word is law. Make it so.

Chapter 29

"My dad raped me!"

Parents, sometimes my job has a lot of positives and then there are the negatives. I have the ability to help guide young alien teen's mind in becoming good law abiding citizens. I also have the authority to save or absolutely destroy their lives when they make bone headed mistakes. I chose to save them. Who knows when one of these aliens' teens will find the cure for cancer or other ills that plague our world.

One of the negatives that come into my office, not often I am happy to say, is when a confused and crying alien teen daughter comes to me and exclaim that she has been raped by her own dad or step-dad.

There are a lot of jokes out there about step-dads being given a bad name. Thank God most of those jokes and sayings are false and fictitious. A dad is either a father or step-father, doesn't matter just as long the love and protect their alien child. Whether the alien child is his or his by way of marrying its' mother.

The hardest part of this type of scenario is the fact that I have to have the alien teen tell me in "details" what occurred and how it happened. Not to mention laying the event out step by step. I attribute the good relationship I have with all of my alien teens that they feel comfortable enough to tell me the details I need to investigate this case.

Fortunately in most of the cases I've had to handle, it was not the biological or step-father that was the culprit. It was usually the live-in boyfriend that was the demon within that family. This my parents should make you sit up and take notice.

Mother's are really blindsided when these type of situations happen within their own home and to their own alien daughters. There are cases of mother's turning a blind eye or a deaf ear to the pleas of an alien daughter who is trying to tell her what is happening.

There are the mother's who "know" this is happening, but they don't want to upset their live-in boyfriend. The last thing they want is for that boyfriend to walk out on her.

You also have the mothers who suspect that something might be happening, but won't go the extra mile to investigate. They are afraid to ask their alien daughter if "this is happening to you" because of fear that the alien daughter will validate her fears. She doesn't want to loose that man.

Alien daughters turn to the only one who will listen to them, their teacher, guidance counselors and their school resource officers. Most of the time, the SRO is their first stop. They know things will happen when they get us on the case. They know we will make all that abuse stop. They understand the school's hands are tied in matters such as this. Their best resource is their counselors who will help them cope mentally while the "ass" of the suspect belong's the law.

The worst part of my interview comes when I have the parent sitting next to the alien daughter and she is "ratting" her mom's man. You can almost feel the mother wants to back hand the alien child and tell her to "shut the hell up, you're lying on my man."

I and talking to the alien daughter, but my other eye is on the parent's reaction. If the parent shows emotions, then she is almost happy that this sordid crime is now off her back and in my hands. She can still be the "good guy" in this situation.

If the parent is in tears and shaking her head in denial, then she definitely knew this rape was taking place, but she is not willing to sacrifice her man because her silly alien daughter is ratting him out.

When the parent's mouth drops open and her eyes become as large as a saucer, then she had no idea that that bastard she thought was her boyfriend has been taking liberties with her own alien child. She usually had that look of "I'm gonna kill that bastard when I get home." That's the spirit mom. But that still does not absolve you of the fact that you should have notice the mental, physical, and emotional change in your alien daughter. Starting right now, the abuse stops.

Nothing gives me more pleasure then to go to a Rapist's job and slap on the silver bracelets. Then the words of "you are under arrest for rape." Seem to ring out loudly for all to hear and to digest. They have been working and laughing right alongside a man that was raping his girlfriend's alien child. Crazy!

Mothers, wake up and remember, you are charged with the protection of your alien child first. You "man" comes second in the equation. Again I must add that this is not all "live-in boyfriends," most are really good people and good providers. They accepts the alien's teens along with the mother as a package deal. Always makes for a good family environment.

But for all of you idiots who have these unsavory minds sets that you can have the mother and the alien daughter to do with what you will sexually, you better think again. I have extra sets of bracelets.

Chapter 30

Senior pranks from Hell

Okay, it really time to lighten things up a bit. As I said before, high school teen aliens can give you things to laugh about for days. Sometimes those things make you go hmmm, but for the most part, you find yourself smiling to yourself as some of the dumbest things under the sun, or under the roof of the high school.

When you are about a month away from graduation, one can almost expect the unexpected to happen. The high school prank is as old as time itself. There have been some great ones over the years and each year, the alien teens try to top the last year's alien graduates.

This is just one of those instances. It was just your usual morning and all of the alien teen was milling about the lobby running their mouths and laughing at nothing. I told the principal that it has been really to quiet for a normal month before graduation. He agreed and said that we should keep our eyes open for anything to happen.

We didn't have long to wait. All of a sudden the lobby erupted with scream, shrieks, yells, and laughter. All at once. The middle of the lobby where the largest concentration of alien teens was standing suddenly parted like the red sea. There were alien students trying to climb on top of other alien students. There were others who ran like their butts were on fire.

There were some that did not run, but were amused about what had just happened. This situation made the biggest of the football players run for cover or try to jump up into the arms of their alien girlfriends. Not an easy feat for an alien girl to carry a 200 lbs alien football player.

The principal and I rushed over to see what had caused this kind of mass hysteria. The fear on some of the alien teens faces showed that this must be some devastating and really scary.

Once we got to the center of the lobby, we were almost bent over laughing at what we discovered. All of the screams and mass panic was caused by crickets. Someone had just released hundreds of chirping, hopping, ugly cricket right in the middle of the alien teen mass.

They were hopping every where and getting on some alien students who ran or screamed bloody murder. Never thought I would see a whole alien football team run or shrink away from a little cricket. But there was the proof. The big sissies were scared to death. The funny part about this whole thing is that all of my white alien teen girls were picking the crickets up with and trying to get other alien students not to step on them or kill them. They had no fear of crickets, especially my redneck alien girls.

Needless to say, they finally rounded all of the crickets up and put them in a bag to protect them from the alien students who wanted to kill them. Wow, they wanted to save the cricket's lives. How noble of these alien girls. One of the alien girl had the bright idea to release them safely into the lake in front of the school. She took them out and poured them out into the lake. Finally they were free of the alien teens.

Silly alien teen girl, she didn't realize fish love to eat crickets. Gulp!

She didn't have the heart to tell her alien girl friends that she had accidentally fed all of the crickets to the fish. Well, what her alien girlfriends don't know, won't hurt them.

Then there was the day I was walking down the hallway just cruising as usual. Suddenly, an alien student burst out of the restroom almost running into me. He said excuse me and then walked rapidly down the hallway.

I can't remember all of the names of my alien students in this school, but I know the majority of them by face. That was not one of our alien students. I called the security guard to be on the look out for the strange alien student and gave a clothing description. He ran out of the restroom pretty quickly for a reason. Matter of fact, a nearby alien girl said to me she wondered why alien Brad was here in this school. He attends school at our cross town sister high school. Hmm.

I went into the restroom and there was the reason he hauled ass out of the area. The security guard had detained him and another alien student in the parking lot. I notified the principal and assistant. In the restroom, in a sink, standing about 10 inches high, was a greenish brown, still steaming pile of "SHIT!"

What the hell kinda' senior prank is this? I will tell you that alien teen must have been saving up for a week to deposit it in the sink. It had to be a relief when he let it go.

The other alien teen that was with him was supposed to be the look out, but he got cold feet and scrammed without telling his friend. He was waiting by the car. Both are now in serious trouble. The bad thing about this scenario, both alien students have been given full scholarships to a prestigious college. You know their parents are gonna' be pissed.

And they were. The alien teen were not allowed to graduate with their senior class. Matter of fact, they were suspended from school and had to serve some probationary time before they could finally receive their diplomas. I took it easy on these knuckleheaded aliens and we gave them some community service work. They had to wash every school bus the county had. Talk about hard labor.

The only real victim in this whole incident was the janitor who was selected to clean that big pile of smelly nasty poop. The first janitor threatened to quit if she had to go in there and fight with that thing. By now it was starting to lean over the edge of the sink, yuck.

Finally one brave janitor was found to go in and deal with the crap. I'm not sure, but I haven't seen that janitor since the day he walked into the restroom armed with a bucket and a pooper scooper. You don't suppose….. nah. I don't think and pile of poop is a match for a big scrapping janitor like the one that went into the restroom.

It's been almost a year now and still no sign of the janitor. The pile of poop is gone also. Hmmm.

Chapter 31

Teen driver's from Hell

As you know parents, the one thing that really make us loose the little bit of hair we have concerning our alien teens is the day they get that driver's license.

When some people use the term, license to kill, they are not talking about Bond, James Bond, they are taking about our alien teens behind the wheel of our cars. That's definitely has make me a little greyer than I want to be. I'm talking about your alien teen's parents, not mine. I'm just now in the process of teaching that alien girl of mind that the road way belongs to all and not just her. "Get out of the middle of the road, not!"

There is nothing like watching your alien teen screeching and sliding into the student parking lot. It's sometimes like watching kids play bumper cars. You could depend on doing at least 2 accident reports a week in high school. Those are the ones that report the accidents, not the one's who simply move their car to the other side of the parking lot if no one saw them hit a car. Pretty sneaky these alien teen drivers.

For the most part, alien teen drivers are actually pretty safe drivers. I'm talking about the alien girls, not you alien boys. You guys suck! You have big engine hoopties and pick truck so high you need a ladder to get inside them. And heaven help you if there is not enough mud on your stump jumper truck. You will go at lunch time and find a mud hole and splash through it. It's wild man, wild.

My alien ladies are really cool and they actually use their rear view mirrors. They still refix their makeup in that mirror, but they will check out their back ends. Gotta' love them.

The alien teens park their cars first thing in the morning and are not allowed to go near them until lunchtime. That's a great rule. I don't have to tell you how many times the alien student parking lot has been "make-out" park.

The alien juniors and seniors can leave the campus at lunch, but the other alien students who are lower classmen don't have that luxury. They see their cars in the morning and then again when it's time to go home. That's a great policy and all of the normal high schools have adopted this rule. It' makes for a safer school parking lot.

I have always told my student aliens that if you get into a vehicle accident on the way to school, don't worry about getting to the school before the bell rings. The ringing of the bell is not that important when you have crashed yours or someone else's ride. Anyway, that is an excused tardy slip anyway. So don't stress about it.

Some aliens don't take me at my words. There was one senior alien girl, let's call her alien Kara. She had been in my class when I lectured about accidents and what to do when they occur. I guess she slept through my class.

The very next day, we got a call from alien Kara that she had just ran into the back of another lady's car on the highway just 1 mile from the school. The principal and I usually go to the accident scene to check on the alien student and to stand in for the parent.

When we got to the scene, alien Kara was no where to be found, but the lady she rammed was all in my face cursing and angry that that "white alien girl" just looked at the torn up rear end of her car and said, "sorry, I got to get to class, I'm going to be late."

Oh you can see what's about to happen with this one. I told the lady that the highway patrol was coming and would handle the accident. It's no sooner said then he drove up.

The first thing he asked was where the other driver is. I told him that she had left the scene of the accident and gone on to school. The trooper simply nodded his head and then began to help the angry lady with her copy of the report.

The principal and I headed back to the school and went about our normal duties. I was anticipating the trooper to arrive here as soon as he had cleared the accident scene. It did not take long for him to appear.

Because the whole darn school seems to be made of glass, when anything with police or deputy on it arrives on campus. The whole alien student body has their faces pressed against the window. They know something not good is about to happen.

When the trooper came in, he came directly to my office. That is the protocol when law enforcement enters a school. They have to coordinate any legal proceedings with me first. I notified the principal that we need alien Kara in my office ASAP. He personally went and got her out of class.

Alien Kara was a really thick white alien with chubby rosy cheeks that showed her emotions. When she entered my office and saw the trooper sitting there. All of the rose in her cheeks fell onto the. Her mouth dropped open and you could almost see a tear appear in the corner of her eye.

The trooper introduced himself and then politely explained what a boneheaded thing she had just done. She nodded her head in agreement and weakly repeated that she didn't want to be late for class. The trooper had the look of understanding, but the law comes first and he will do his job.

After the talking was done, he had her stand up and place her hands behind her back. Alien Kara's legs grew very weak suddenly as she realized that she was being arrested. The trooper said he was taking her for leaving the scene of an accident with minor injuries. Dummy, she didn't even ask the lady if she was hurt out there.

She was escorted down the hallway, through a hallway full of alien students who were changing class at that particular moment. The tears really flowed, but the law is the law. You just knew everyone and their friends were texting each other about who they just saw going to jail.

And to jail she went. I allowed her parents to pick her car up from the parking lot. No need to pile on as alien Kara has enough on her plate right now.

She spent the night in jail. She made bond the next morning. Fortunately, she was able to graduate with no problems. After all, it was still just a traffic problem and not a felony. This was still enough of a wake up to the other alien teens about staying put at accidents.

Parents, the best thing you can do for your alien child is get them into drivers training when it's available. Let the gym teacher get the grey hair as she tries to keep your alien teen from running into ditches and hitting others cars. That's what she is paid for. Plus they will be using the school's driver's Ed car and not yours. Good deal.

The worst thing your alien teen can do is to load up their car with other aliens. This is when trouble is sure to follow. They are running their mouths, laughing and playing like there is no tomorrow. Not only that, the music is booming loud cause the alien driver has put the family stereo speaker in the trunk of the car for that rich, booming sound. You know, the kind of sound that rattles the trunk and cost you a doctor's bill when they suffer hearing loss.

We call this "distracted driving." Anything that takes your attention off of the road and makes you look down, back, sideways is gonna' cost you dearly.

The worst method of distracted driving is done by alien teens and adults on cell phones. They totally forget they have to steer the car when the phone conversation has gotten good. You see the idiots. They have their heads tilted over towards their shoulders and looks to be driving their cars sideways. I see it so many times happening in rush hour.

The distracted phone driver will actually see the car in front of them have stopped, they know it has stopped, but because their attention is more fully on the phone conversation, they cannot react quickly enough to hit the brakes. Crash! That's not the sound of your car hitting the rear of another car, that's the sound of your bank account level hitting bottom after paying all of those medical bills of the other driver.

In the mornings, alien teens sometimes get to school early to meet their alien friends. They get together so they may leave and to Mikey D's for breakfast. I personally think that breakfast at the school is pretty good. Almost like good country cooking. They have grits. Yum.

After all of the alien teens had piled into the 1988 Buick, they headed for the exit gate of the school. They were laughing and tripping, and of course thumping the music loud. There were 4 aliens in the car. It's about a good 300 feet from the school to the front gate.

Once the alien teen driver got to the gate, he looked right, then hit the gas to make a left turn up the road and to Mikey D's they go. They didn't make it there.

The security guard had just drove up to position himself to direct traffic at the entrance gate as he does every morning. He did not expect to witness what was about to happen this particular morning.

He came across the walkie talkie with a frantic voice, almost like he was screaming about something. I told him to calm down and say again. He did. What he said was that a Ford F-150 pick up truck heading south on the road in front of the school's gate had just plowed into a car load of alien students. He said it was pretty bad!

I grabbed the principal and jumped into my patrol car and sped out to the gate. There it was, the pickup truck had "T-boned" the Buick on the driver's side of the car. The car for the most part took the hit pretty good. After all, they use to build them pretty sturdy in the 80's. One of the alien teens was laying on the pavement, not moving and barely breathing. One of the school's teacher, who was there when the "hit" happen, was cradling his head in her lap.

Another teen alien was walking around, shaking and just plain looking like he saw a ghost. I had him sit down until we find out if he has any unknown injuries. The other two aliens, one the driver, only had minor cuts and bumps. They seemed to be alright as they were on those darn cell phones hollering for their mommies to come and get them. No matter how old an alien teen gets, he will always cry for his mommy when something bad happens.

I got the ambulance enroot to us and it showed up within 8 minutes as the station was just up the road. They put the one alien teen on a stretcher and prepared to transport him to the hospital. He was stirring slightly which was a good sign. The other aliens refused to go to the hospital and wanted to go to the school and wait for mommy to pick them up. They all will be pretty sore tomorrow. That's how the body works. To protect itself from injury and pain, the brain will actually route pain and stress to another part of the body for now. The minute you are relaxed and home, it's like the brains says, "Okay, remember that pain I tucked away in the corner earlier? Well here it is, and you are welcome to it."

It comes back with a vengeance. In some cases, you may not even be able to get out of bed. Been there, done that, not a good thing. Be that as it may, the body and mind is a wonderful piece of work. Wonder who designed it?

Parents take heed after you finish reading this passage. It's up to you as well as me to teach our alien teens about the safe way to operate that 2 or 4 ton piece of metal. By teaching Them well and staying on top of their driving habits, that family car won't be their all metal casket. Enough said parents.

Chapter 32

The Bully from Hell

Face it parents, not only do all of these new high schools have everything that a modern alien teen would want, but they also come with a couple of things that they don't want or need. We have all had to deal with this "pox" at one time in our school lives. Some of you are dealing with it as we speak on your job. The problem is that we can't "shoot" the problem and make it go away. Well, I can, but that still would not be right to do.

The Bully has been around for centuries, just like the cockroach. They evolve and multiply, but they will always be with us. Some of you guys out there reading this book use to be bullies. Some are you probably are still bullies today.

Bullies come in all shapes, sizes, color, and sex. Their only reason for existing is to create hell for you and others that don't have as hard a life as he or she does. Sometimes bullies are just stupid and don't realize it. Only when someone brave enough to tell that idiot "what is what," and survive, do the bully finally see the light. Actually the best thing or the best way to get rid of a bully is to get all your friends together and "kick the living shit out of his or her ass." Sorry weak hearted Readers, but I needed to get that out there.

Alien teens have to suffer the harassment bullies heap upon them sometimes throughout their school life. I have to admit, the schools have done a pretty good job of combating the bully thing. The problem is that some alien teens are afraid to tell on the bully. The bully has threatened to kick their ass if they tell the cop in school or the principal.

Most alien teens understand that while they are in school, they are protected. But when the bully lives and breaths in the same neighborhood, then it is sometime better to keep the lips zipped. I wish we could have cops on every corner and at every bus stop, but we can't. That is why we still rely on the alien teen to find the courage to turn in the bully and let me do my thing.

Believe it or not parents, most of the bullies in high school nowadays are not the alien teen boys, but the alien teen girls. As you know, alien girls are very dangerous things loaded with estrogen. They will not only talk about ripping your head off, they will lay hands on and try to do it.

I don't have to tell you how many times the janitors have had to pick up left over "weave" from a good alien girl fight. Usually It's one alien girl who was bullying another. It finally came to a head. I always preach to the alien students that you have but to come to me and identify who the bully is and I will become the "bully."

Not only that, I will be the bully to their parents also. The last thing a bully wants to have happen is a cop showing up at their parents door and "bringing him out!"

I let the parent know what it's gonna' cost their alien child and them in monetary value if the alien student the bully is harassing is harmed or continued to be bullied. You really don't want to "test" me at my word when I tell you the 411. That's when the parent will call the bully and threatened them. My job here is done. Then I will tell the bully, "I will be watching you." Not quite like "Arnold," but just as effective.

You have always heard that a bully is someone who is misunderstood. He is seeking attention that he is not getting from home. Bull. A bully is an idiot with no brains and they should get a life. We have no time for someone to harass good alien teens who are trying to get the education they need to be "someone" someday.

I have no patience or love for these poxes in school and have always done my best to eliminate this type of scum. If I succeed in getting them at least placed on legal probation, then all the more better. The next thing he or she does something stupid, they are heading down to the "big house."

Parents, heed my warning if your alien teen has been identified by the school administrators as a bully. We will take the time to try and work with you out of respect. If we don't see a change in your alien bully, then his ass is grass. He will be living in this high school on borrow time.

Wanna be gang members are the truest form or bullies. They are always trying to recruit new members for their gang or local groups. Those alien teens who know better than to join are then harassed and threatened bodily harm. I wish a Mutha' would threaten one of the alien teens I am sworn to protect.

Suffice to say, if these wanna be gang members/bullies want to die at the tender age of 15, then they will die alone. We will not let you peace loving alien teen have to put up with this nonsense. We have a "war on gangs" are we are coming for them all very soon.

Parents, let us know if your alien teen has been or is being bullied. We want to "bully" them back and see if they can handle it.

Chapter 33

Prom night

It's here finally, the night that all of the alien senior teens have been waiting 4 long years for, prom night. Or as it's known to most of us administrators, "what's keep that prom gown up" night. It is a wondrous time and it's a nightmare to plan

I give my props to the teacher drafted to walk the plank and put together a good prom night. The pulling together of the theme, materials, the building, the food, the chaperones and on and on is truly something to behold, as well as fear.

Over the years, there have been some very good proms, some not so good ones. The alien seniors are really mindful of how their prom looks and want to go out with a bang. Particular attention is paid to the overall look of the decorations. Heaven help the prom coordinator if the dance floor is too small. Can't "back that booty up" on a dance floor that is only made for midgets.

When the prom coordinator does a good job, the alien seniors will complain that something was wrong. When something is wrong, well they complain even more. Anyway you put it, the prom coordinator is the "goat' when it comes to trying to please the school administrators and the alien seniors.

Be it a hotel, a restaurant, a warehouse, a museum or the school lobby, how these schools make due with almost nothing is simply amazing. They can actually transform nothing into something special. Alien seniors aside, you are a great creator Ms. Prom coordinator.

Then there's the alien seniors themselves. They run all around the city looking and trying on tuxes and dresses. They invade every Asian nail place in the area to get the fingers and toes looking their best. They hit the shoe store and boutiques looking for the highest, skinniest pair of heels the store has. 4 inches are for amateurs from what I hear.

What size you wear alien senior girl? A size 9? Okay. What's that, you want a size 7 ½? You will "make" it fit? Well okay. That's call a "can do" spirit of the prom.

The alien senior guys have laid out a great amount of money for limos or have put a mirror shine on their personal cars. The fat 26 inch rims are glistening in the sun light. Some alien seniors will have their poor old dads act as the chauffeur. That's okay. They are happy for the experience and filled with pride when their alien senior makes a splash getting out of the ride.

The hair styles are piled as high as Marge Simpson's and some have actually grown 5 feet longer magically. Believe me, Mr. Ray's house of weave is plum out of hair piece no. 8.

The faculty had gotten their instructions and are listed on the form as to what shift they will work. It's usually run in two shifts. Most teachers would rather be on the first shift to get it over with. I, myself will be there for the duration along with the other administrators. Not that we are gluttons for punishment, but because we care that everything flows nicely and everyone has a good time. Most of all, everyone is safe and enjoying themselves. Of course we do have to restrict the areas in which they can roam. No making out at this year's prom. Oh no, not gonna' happen here.

Finally the day is gone and 8:00 p.m. rolls around. You can bet that no one will show up at the opening of the doors. Alien seniors have spent a fortune on the limos, the clothing and make-up, so it would be a waste of a good "grand entrance" to get there before anyone can really see them. The faculty and staff don't count.

Slowly they begin to file in. Each alien senior girl's prom dress is more lovely then the next one. And the mystery still remain, what is holding that prom dress up and in place. We guess the senior alien girls are using "duct tape." That will hold anything in place.

Each dress is an awesome sight. The colors are splendid and bright. Every so often you get a short prom dress, and I do mean short. Alien girl, what the hell are you wearing, Tarzan's loin cloth? Now you know you will not be able to attend this prom with all of your "goodies" hanging out like that.

That alien senior girl's prom dress was a brown two piece loin cloth with bra. With each step she took heading back to the car she exposed her matching thong. Ah, but these alien senior girls know what time it is. She had a matching shawl in the car. She wrapped up in the shawl and made her entrance again. This time, a little more respectable.

"Hey Mr. Cardoorears, I'll bet your salary against mine, that the shawl disappears as soon as she is inside the prom area." He did not want to take that bet. After all, we know our alien senior girls well.

The alien guys were the "bomb!" They have changed from wearing pants that hung below their asses to respectable, professional looking gentlemen in their suits and tuxes. It's simply amazing to find these good looking men hidden inside of an alien shell.

Once inside, the comparisons are made, all of the compliments are passed out and then it's time. "Dee Jay, hit the jams and make it funky." The music comes alive now that the elevator music is done. I saw the principal give the sign to kick it "ol skool."

The alien senior ran to the floor as if something was for sale at a discount. They got their dance on and the fun has really started. I was waiting on the sideline thinking, any minute now, the "real dancing" will begin.

My prediction was not far off. The music changed to one of today's favorite jam and the alien seniors really came alive. All of those high heel pumps were left on the floor under the tables. It time to get barefooted and loose. The hats and canes are laid across the tables.

There it goes! The first senior alien girl pulled her prom dress up to about her thigh area, bent over and started working her ass up against the crotch of her date. The alien date stood there with his hips thrust forwards so his alien girl date could "feel" him. They were working it on the dance floor. So were almost half the alien seniors on the floor. Even the white alien girls tried to "get" some of that action, though they have not quite mastered the gyrations like the black alien senior girls. They gave it their best shot.

There goes the chaperones into action. I said, there goes the chaperones into action. Well how do you like that? There is no effort to stop this orgy of bumping and grinding on the dance floor. The fact is, as soon as you separate one couple of alien seniors, ten more will be doing the forbidden dance. It's a no win situation. So let the senior aliens have their fun. This is after all, the last night that they will all be together as this year's family. Can't remember anyone getting pregnant from dancing anyway, so let it ride! Nobody's getting hurt.

Chapter 34

Graduation

Being a parent myself, I can tell you that I am actually looking forward to my alien daughter graduating and making her way to college where she will cost me a fortune to keep her there. You too will know the same feeling as soon as your alien teens walk that isle as professional wrestler Rick Flair use to say.

With the prom orgy out of the way the next thing your alien teens are commanded to do is pay up or don't graduate. Any lost books or damage to the lab equipment has to be paid for. No one escapes the dreaded school accountant and her trusty calculator.

The other problem that the alien teens are trying to cope with is the fact that they aren't gonna' graduate. What's that you say? Thats' is right. There are some of your alien teens that have played around, didn't go to class or skipped school altogether that will not have their names on the roll of graduates.

It's amazing how all year there are alien teens that wasted time and didn't care about keeping tabs on their grades. But there they are, crowding into the guidance office begging the counselor to find a way to make it across the stage in June.

It never fails that these alien teens don't have a sense of urgency until they see all of their friends checking out colleges and making plans for after school. Suddenly, they want to know if they have enough credits to get that coveted diploma. When told they will not graduate, the first thing they want to do is blame the teachers and get the parents involved. Parents, don't get drawn into this effort to bully the guidance to help your lazy alien teen a free pass.

The fun begins after finding out that they are not graduating, they have to scramble and find ways of making up credits they didn't work for. There are several ways to make up some of those credits if there aren't too many missing.

Credit retrieval is one way as well as on-line courses. They require the lazy alien teen that wouldn't come to school during normal days, now they must come to school on Saturdays until told to stop. I think that is a just punishment. Each Saturday I would see all of the little alien faces in the class working like little bees in the hive.

Some of them will do enough to make it to G-day. Others will again not make the grade. This is what's wrong with our alien teens that don't have a real parent riding their asses and making sure they are doing what is necessary. You would think that after your alien teen left middle school, they would have more common sense and be more responsible. Then again, here they are in class on a nice Saturday morning while all of their alien friends are out having fun and planning their new lives

The teachers and guidance counselors have a hard job and do their jobs very well. Sometimes they are swimming up stream when the alien teen is not cooperating with them to help them realize what they need to do. I have seen the frustration on their faces when even they know it's a waste of time fooling with a teen alien that don't care about his own future.

When the smoke finally clears, the final list of graduates is set and for the most part, those alien teens already know they have made the grade. They have ordered their expensive invitations and are working on getting the also expensive yearbooks signed by other alien's friends.

There are rehearsals and more rehearsals in the gym and the auditorium. The activity coordinator is stressed as usual. She has a feeling of doom and gloom that won't go away until the G-day is over. The last thing she needs to happen is someone is actually naked under their grad gowns. Then again there are the ones that like to smuggle cool things under their gowns to throw out later during the ceremony.

I tell you that I witness one high school's graduation and it seems as if half of the female alien students had sneaked beach balls in under their gowns. Then again, they were all just pregnant. Guess they wanted to get a head start on starting that family before going off to college. Then again, that unborn child will probably be raised by the grandmother. She just doesn't realize it yet.

The day of the graduation is a hectic day and everyone is looking really nice. They are all lined up and ready for the coordinator to give the sign for the music to start. Pomp and circumstance is blaring from a lone piano and the alien students take a deep breath. They are about to be alien students and high schoolers for only 2 more hours. The auditorium is filled to capacity and the crowd is yelling out their alien's names.

The announcement was to keep cool when the alien student enter and keep this ceremony traditionally quiet and nice. But you know there are some idiots who arrived late and missed the whole speech about acting like an asshole at the graduation. Never fails.

Of course, the whole auditorium is surrounded with cops everywhere. You don't know if they are there because someone is threatened to kidnap the graduating aliens or if they didn't have anything else to do that day. Take your pick.

The ceremony is rather quick and all of the dry ass speeches are finished. I will never know why some schools have a need to have 50 different alien students sing songs that have nothing to do with the graduation. To me it takes away from what we are here to accomplish.

One of the funniest parts of graduation is the superintendent. Depending on how many schools are graduating in his district, he may say the same speech a total of 5 or 10 times. He should know it by heart by the 4 time he gives that same speech. I know the cops that are there all day have learned to tune the speech out.

The alien students make their way across the stage and get that graduation folder, which doesn't have the actual diploma in it, but gives the alien student a thrill anyway. They will pick up the real diploma later down stairs. Some school will mail it to them. That's a good thing to have lost in the mail.

The administrators are positioned right near the end of the graduation ramp just in case a newly graduated alien teen wants to do a cart wheel or bust a little "breaking" move. Maybe do the "krump" in celebration of getting that folder. No one is brave enough to do anything but wave and keep moving. That's the whole idea.

The final word is given and the tassels are turned signifying that these alien teens are now young alien graduates. Welcome to the world of the unemployed. Hope you like it here, cause you can never leave.

The after celebration is a great sight to behold as the parents are waiting outside to hug and take pictures for days. Smiles and grins are all over the place. It's time to head to the nearest restaurant and have a celebration dinner. Yes good times are all around. They all enjoy this day and it may even be celebrated tomorrow, but sooner or later, the reality that the alien teen is not a child anymore will sink in.

The next day when you as the parent wake that new adult alien sleeping in your bed in your house, you will meet with some resistance as the alien adult tells you that they don't have a reason to get up. They don't have to go to school, so why not just lay here until you call them for breakfast. You know this will happen to you, not all of you, but to some.

A lot of alien adults will have a heavy heart and be touched with a lingering touch of sadness knowing that the life they use to know is a thing of the past now. They will realize that they cannot count on you the way they did in the old. They will have to fend for themselves and whether they succeed or fail, they are their own alien person.

Whether going to college, the military or entering the work force, your former alien child will have to choose which course is best suited to them. I will be seeing some of the aliens in my capacity as a cop. Those aliens too will have made a decision. A stupid one, but still a decision nevertheless.

Graduation, the time when that little 7 lbs. of flesh walks out of your door and makes it's own way in the world. Well look at it this way parents. Now you can finally clean that extra room really good and rent it out to a real paying customer. Enough said.

Chapter 35

Final Words

And there you have it my fellow parents a little insight into the life and times of your alien teen during their high school years. The good thing about the life of and alien teen is that most of the year, they are actually involved with education. They are actually sitting there, listening to the knowledge the low paid teacher is trying to impart.

I can honestly say that out of 2,400 alien teens in any high school these days, there are only a hand full of alien teens that do the "wrong" thing or try to take short cuts that end up with bad results.

I commend all of you parents who have alien teens that bring those A's and B's home each exam period. That proves that you have done a great job early in the life of your alien teen. You have instilled a sense of priority and dedication. Nothing pleases us more then to have a alien teen throw their arms around us laughing and happy because they made the honor roll or had nothing on their report lower then a B. They make us so proud of them.

Parents, I am very proud of you for creating such a fine alien teen. The school faculty and administrators are with your alien teens more hours and days of the year then you are at times. We actually come to know your child better then you sometimes. This is due to the fact that, while home, they will only show you the behaved side. When they are in high school around us, they show the behaved side, the social side, as well as the naughty side.

We don't have the ability to ground them or take away their TV. That's why they will sometimes pull the wool over your eyes by faking goodness.

Parents, we understand that these alien teens come from various economical backgrounds. There is nothing that we can do about that, but in high school, all alien teen are on a level playing field. We don't care if you have a BMW or a Pinto in the parking lot, you each will get the same great chance at an education.

We make it a point to not see your financial status here. We don't care if you vacation in the Hampton's or can only afford Myrtle Beach. Your alien teen is special and will be treated with that same special care.

One thing I really love about high school teens is the fact that they don't see "color" like we of the old skool days do. Whether you are black, white, yellow, or green, every alien teen is treated equally and fairly. This is the hallmark of a great run high school.

By the same token, I commend the alien teens themselves, they truly are the future. They will one day make it possible not to see race or color because they will produce offspring's that will connect us all together. The race box on applications for employment will finally disappear forever. These teen alien will make us for the most part, one race, the human race. Keep it up alien teens and always be color blind. This makes you more intelligent then us, the parents and adults will ever be.

Finally, enjoy this book parents. Read it then pass it to your friends and family. Sometimes it's funny. Sometimes it's tragic. Most of the time, it's just alien teens working a parent's last nerve.

End.

About the Author

The author of "Parents, your High School Teens have been replaced by Aliens" is a current Law Enforcement Officer. He is a former School Resource Officer, Sheriff's Deputy and aspiring author and Investigator. He is a 14 year veteran in Law Enforcement.

Born Odell P. Glenn, the author is a graduate of Winnsboro High School, located in a little town called Winnsboro, SC. His former school now goes by the name Fairfield Central High School. That shows how things have changed in the small town located just 20 north of Columbia, SC.

Odell is a 20 Army veteran having served in many capacities while a member of the armed services. Those to includes jobs positions with the United States Army Signal Corps, the Military Intelligence Command, Germany, the Military Police, U.S. Army Recruiting Command, White House Communications, DC.

Odell is the father to a beautiful child, named Zahtia, 16, but thinks she's 21. She is real reason he decided to write this book. He has seen how his daughter has changed from the little girl with curls to a young woman trying to figure out who she is and what she wants to become. We all experience this with our teens as they grow up.

"Read it, laugh at it, be shocked by it, but enjoy it anyway."

Odell P. Glenn